APPLICATION CASES IN MIS
Using Spreadsheet and Database Software (3.5" Version)

Second Edition

James N. Morgan
Northern Arizona University

IRWIN
Chicago • Bogotá • Boston • Buenos Aires • Caracas
London • Madrid • Mexico City • Sydney • Toronto

Richard D. Irwin makes no warranties, either expressed or implied, regarding the enclosed Computer software package, its merchantability or its fitness for any particular purpose. The exclusion of implied warranties is not permitted by some states. The exclusion may not apply to you. This warranty provides you with specific legal rights. There may be other rights that you may have which may vary from state to state. ©Richard D. Irwin Inc., 1990.

©Richard D. Irwin, a Times Mirror Higher Education Group, Inc. company, 1993 and 1996

All rights reserved. No part of this publication may be reproduced, stored in a retieval system, or transmitted, in any form or by any means, electronic, mechanical photocopying, recording, or otherwise, without the prior written permission of the publisher.

Printed in the United States of America.

ISBN 0-256-22056-5 (3.5 Version)

IBM and IBM PC are registered trademarks of International Business Corporation.
Microsoft and Windows are registered trademarks of Microsoft Corporation.
Lotus and 1-2-3 are registered trademarks of the Lotus Development Corporation.
Excel is a trademark of Microsoft Corporation

1 2 3 4 5 6 7 8 9 0 WCB 3 2 1 0 9 8 7 6

PREFACE

Application Cases in MIS: Using Spreadsheet and Database Software was written to support any MIS textbook that is used for courses which have a substantial hands-on component. This casebook is designed to assist students in learning to design and develop hands-on computer applications to solve managerial problems. It is written for students who are prospective managerial users of computer systems, and not for potential IS professionals. The cases presented in this casebook are business oriented, because this casebook is intended primarily for use by students majoring in a business field. However, the methods and skills covered here should be useful to anyone working in a managerial level professional capacity in any type of organization.

The primary goal of this casebook is to help students learn to design and develop computer applications which use common end user software packages to solve real world managerial problems. The cases presented here are designed to be solved using common spreadsheet or database management packages. While there are no cases in this book centered on work with word processing packages, several of the exercises require students to "incorporate" selected results of a spreadsheet or database application in a letter or memorandum. In those instances, students should use a word processing package to write the letter or memorandum, and should import or "link" the necessary spreadsheet or database results into their word processing document. Instructors may want to further reinforce their students word processing skills by requiring the use of a word processor to complete all written portions of each case they assign.

This casebook is designed for use in classes where incoming students are expected to have some prior experience with the use of spreadsheet and database packages. Thus, the mechanics of using spreadsheet and database software packages are not covered in this casebook. However, only a minimal level of knowledge of the mechanics of spreadsheet and database operations are required to complete the cases presented here. Students entering the course with no previous experience in the use of spreadsheet or database packages will need to use supplementary materials, such as reference manuals or tutorial workbooks, to develop a minimal level of mechanical skills for the packages they will be using.

Students enter MIS courses with widely varied levels of experience in the other functional areas of business. The cases presented in this casebook have been designed to present real world business situations without requiring the use of advanced functional area skills that some students may not have. Brief explanations are provided when basic terminology or calculations based on functional area knowledge are used.

Building end user applications requires more than simply having a knowledge of spreadsheet and database packages. The end user developer must be able to identify situations calling for the development of an end user computer application and must be able to design and develop an application which will provide the appropriate information in as effective a manner as possible. These skills in identifying problem situations requiring computer applications and designing solutions are key to successful use of computer technology, and form the main thrust of this case book.

Two sets of cases are presented: one for spreadsheet applications and one for database applications. The set of database cases also includes some cases requiring the integrated use of both database and spreadsheet software. A chapter of material describing development tools and methods and applying them to a sample case is presented before each set of cases. The chapter materials describing development tools and methods have been rewritten for the second edition to support the use of Windows based spreadsheet and database packages. Each set of cases is designed to help students learn these application development skills. The cases present real world problem situations in a narrative form. Application designs are presented for the first five cases in each set to help give students a better feel for the design process. However, the last five cases in each set require the student to design and develop an appropriate application based only upon the narrative problem description.

Many simple end user database applications can be developed using only a single database table. However, more complex database applications require the development of multiple related tables. This casebook focuses primarily upon single

Application Cases in MIS

table database applications and all of the cases are designed so that they can be completed using a single table. However, in the second edition, coverage of multi-table database applications is provided and five of the database cases are designed with optional multi-table elements.

The windows based "suites" of application development software packages now available have simplified the process of building applications that use multiple tools (e.g. spreadsheet, database, and word processing) in an integrated fashion. Several of the cases in the second edition require an integration solution utilizing two or more software packages.

A data disk is provided to accompany this casebook. The data disk provides partially completed spreadsheet and database files for use on those cases requiring the use of substantial amounts of data. These files are provided in order to reduce the amount of repetitive data entry required to complete these cases. The data disk is designed to be usable on almost all personal computer systems using any of a number of popular commercial spreadsheet and database packages. The system hardware and software requirements to use the data disk are presented below along with a set of instructions for creating a working data disk.

System Requirements

In order to use this casebook effectively, students must have access to:

1. Spreadsheet software that can accept files created by Lotus 123 or EXCEL.

2. Database software that can accept files created by DBASE or ACCESS.

3. A microcomputer with enough memory to operate the software listed above.

Creating a Working Data Disk

There is a data disk which comes with this casebook. This data disk provides files containing the data for many of the cases which can be used to minimize the need for tedious data entry. To ensure that you do not lose or destroy the data on your data disk, you should make a working copy of the data disk and save the original as a backup copy. Follow the appropriate instructions below to create a working data disk before you begin the hands-on operations described in this casebook.

If you have a system with two floppy diskettes -

1. Insert the data diskette that came with your casebook in drive A.

2. Insert a blank formatted diskette in drive B.

3. At the DOS prompt (**A:**) type the command **COPY A:*.* B:**

4. Set aside your casebook diskette and use the copy you just made as your working data disk.

If you have a system with a hard disk -

1. Insert the data diskette that came with your casebook in drive A.

2. At the DOS prompt (**C:**) type **DISKCOPY A: A:**
   The casebook diskette is the *source* disk for this copying operation.

3. When you are prompted to place the *destination* disk in drive A, remove your casebook diskette and replace it with a blank unformatted diskette which you will be using as a working data disk.

4. Continue swapping the casebook or *source* diskette and your blank *destination* diskette as directed until the copy is completed.

5. Set aside your casebook diskette and use the copy you just made as your working data disk.

TABLE OF CONTENTS

CHAPTER 1: DEVELOPING SPREADSHEET APPLICATIONS   1

    The Western Water Company Case   1
    Analysis and Design   2
    Layout Forms - A Basic Design Tool   5
    Coding   9
    Testing Methods   10
    Documentation   10
    Designing Spreadsheets with Multiple Sections   11
    Summary   13

CHAPTER 2: SPREADSHEET CASES   17

    CASE 1: Daydreams Day Care Centers   17
    CASE 2: Bader Products   23
    CASE 3: Howard's Steak House   27
    CASE 4: Hot Pepper Mexican Restaurant   33
    CASE 5: Currier Cams   38
    CASE 6: Point Landes City Government   44
    CASE 7: Datius Software Corporation   47
    CASE 8: Ron's Restaurant Supplies   52
    CASE 9: Alderson for Men   55
    CASE 10: Numismania   59

CHAPTER 3: DEVELOPING DATABASE APPLICATIONS 65

    Characteristics of Spreadsheet and Database Applications   65
    The Tees Are We Case   69
    Analysis   70
    Design   73
    Data Dictionary Forms   74
    Layout Forms   78
    Coding   79
    Testing Methods   81
    Documentation   82
    Integrated Applications   82
    Building Multi-Table Applications   84
    Summary   88

CHAPTER 4: DATABASE CASES 91

    CASE 1: Bunyon Logging Supplies   91
    CASE 2: The Journal-Tribune Corporation   98
    CASE 3: Al's Affordable Autos   106
    CASE 4: Knotty Pine Corporation   114
    CASE 5: Currier Cams - Database   121
    CASE 6: Teen Temps   130
    CASE 7: Ron's Restaurant Supplies - Database   136
    CASE 8: Kwik Shop Movie Rentals   141
    CASE 9: Grand Grounds Incorporated   147
    CASE 10: Pace Picnic Products   151

CHAPTER 1: DEVELOPING SPREADSHEET APPLICATIONS

End user applications can vary greatly in scope and complexity. Some applications simply require the development of a single spreadsheet for one time use by a single user. At the other extreme, end users now often develop application systems involving multiple users accessing sensitive data which must be maintained for repeated use. Clearly, the need for an extensive set of design procedures is more extensive for the latter type of application.

In this chapter we will describe some design tools and methods that are useful even for very simple spreadsheet applications. We will be assuming that the applications we are designing have only one direct user, do not have extensive data storage and control requirements, and are applications which can appropriately be developed using a spreadsheet package. Other design tools and methods appropriate for use with more complex types of applications will be discussed later in this casebook.

The development process for simple end user applications can be viewed as having three components:

1. Analysis and Design
2. Coding
3. Testing and Documentation.

In the sections below we will present a sample case of a problem that can be addressed by a simple spreadsheet application and then describe how such an application might be developed.

THE WESTERN WATER COMPANY CASE

The Western Water Company has used a two-tier price structure for its industrial customers which was designed to encourage water usage. Industrial customers have paid 9 cents a gallon for the first 100,000 gallons used each month, and 7 cents per gallon for each gallon beyond the first 100,000.

Because of a water shortage in the area, and increasing consumer pressure, Western is planning to change its rate structure to one that encourages water conservation. The plan is to retain the two-tier pricing structure, but reverse the tiers so that a higher rate is paid for gallons used beyond some cutoff level. For example, the rates might simply be reversed so that customers would be charged 7 cents a gallon for the first 100,000 gallons and 9 cents a gallon for all additional gallons. Another possible rate structure might be 6 cents a gallon for the first 50,000 gallons and 9.5 cents for all additional gallons. The new rate structure should produce approximately the same revenue as the previous structure. It is important for Western to know how the new rate structure affects individual industrial customers, since opposition can be expected from any customers whose water costs are substantially increased. Western has asked us to create a spreadsheet model which will allow the analysis of the impact of alternative rates and cutoff levels.

Although the price changes are designed to reduce water use Western does not have a good estimate of how much reduction will occur. Therefore, for the purpose of this spreadsheet analysis, we will assume that the number of gallons used by each customer is unaffected by the changes in the rate structure.

ANALYSIS AND DESIGN

Analysis of a potential end user application addresses the fundamental components of an information system: input, processing, output, storage, and control. Figure 1-1 provides a pictorial representation of these system components and the questions they address. In analyzing a potential application, attention focuses first on the *output* to be produced by the application. What information is needed and in what form should it be presented? Next we must look at the *input* data to be supplied to the application. What data are available? from what sources? and in what form? Then we must examine the *processing* requirements. What operations or transformation processes will be required to convert the available inputs into the desired output? Among software packages which the developer is able to use, which package can best perform the operations required? We may find that the desired output cannot be produced from the inputs that are available. If this is the case we must either make

Developing Spreadsheet Applications

Figure 1-1

The Components of an Information System

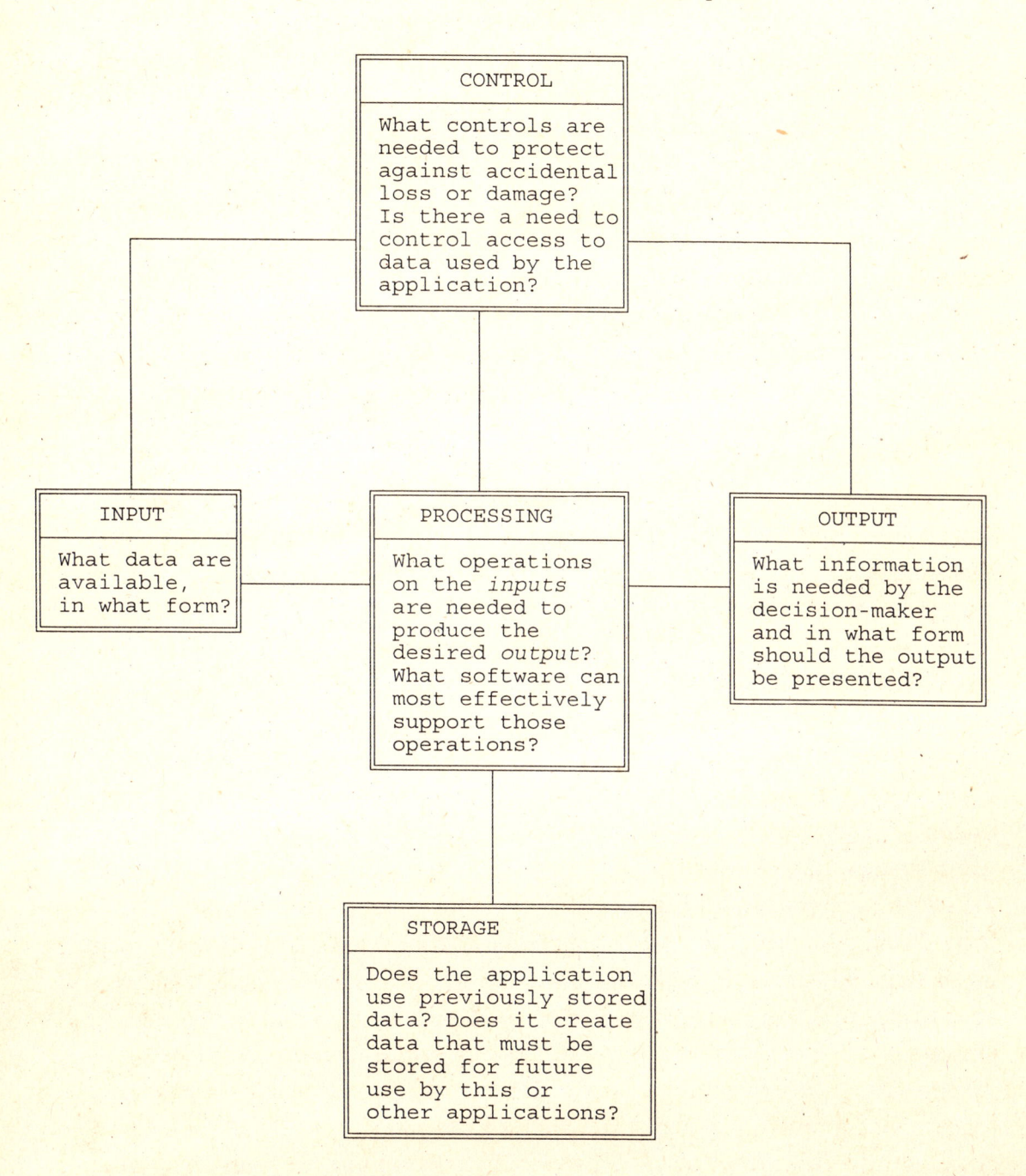

```
                    ┌─────────────────────┐
                    │       CONTROL       │
                    ├─────────────────────┤
                    │ What controls are   │
                    │ needed to protect   │
                    │ against accidental  │
                    │ loss or damage?     │
                    │ Is there a need to  │
                    │ control access to   │
                    │ data used by the    │
                    │ application?        │
                    └─────────────────────┘
```

INPUT	PROCESSING	OUTPUT
What data are available, in what form?	What operations on the *inputs* are needed to produce the desired *output*? What software can most effectively support those operations?	What information is needed by the decision-maker and in what form should the output be presented?

```
                    ┌─────────────────────┐
                    │       STORAGE       │
                    ├─────────────────────┤
                    │ Does the application│
                    │ use previously stored│
                    │ data? Does it create│
                    │ data that must be   │
                    │ stored for future   │
                    │ use by this or      │
                    │ other applications? │
                    └─────────────────────┘
```

adjustments to the output we expect to produce or find additional sources of input data. The fundamental elements of input, processing, and output are present in all applications.

Storage and *control* elements may not be required for some small scale applications. Applications which require extensive use of stored data or the creation of data which must be stored for future use are better suited to database development. Thus, in this chapter we will assume that our applications do not require a distinct, formal, storage element. We will describe the storage element in conjunction with our discussion of development methods for database applications in Chapter 3.

Necessary control measures for applications vary greatly depending upon the: scope and duration of the application, the number and nature of the users of the application, and the nature of the data involved. For the application presented here and the cases presented in Chapter 2, we will be assuming that no special procedures to restrict access to data are needed. We will also assume that each application will be utilized either by one individual serving as a developer/user or by a developer and a single additional user. Control measures will be needed to protect against accidental loss or damage to an application file. The most basic protection against this type of loss is simply to *make backup copies of application files on a frequent, and systematic basis*. If a spreadsheet application is to be used on a repeated basis or used by an individual other than its developer, it is important to *use the cell protection features of spreadsheet software to protect key cells from accidental erasure*.

When PCs are connected to a network, a decision must be made about where to locate an application. The most appropriate location decision for an end user developed application which designed to serve a large number of users over a long period of time may be to place the application on a network file server. If this is to be done, there should be a common set of standards with respect to quality and control which must be met before applications are placed on the server. In this book we will assume that all of the applications are limited enough in scope and number of users affected that they should be maintained on the PCs of the users involved.

Developing Spreadsheet Applications

LAYOUT FORMS - A BASIC DESIGN TOOL

The output requirements of applications are often depicted visually through layout forms. A layout form is simply a mock-up of what a report or screen should look like. It shows titles and headings for rows and columns along with either sample data or descriptions of the data that are to be presented in the report. In the case of spreadsheets, input, output, and processing activities are intermingled in a single spreadsheet file. A layout form can be used to record the input, processing, and output requirements of a spreadsheet application like that required by Western Water Company.

Figure 1-2 shows a layout form for our sample application. In general, the portions of the layout form enclosed in boxes or referenced by arrows contain samples or descriptions of what is to appear on the actual report. Nonboxed areas contain literal labels and values as they are to appear on the report.

Define Title and Heading Labels

We begin by selecting an appropriate title and then creating heading labels for the columns of data that need to be reported for each customer (the column headings under estimated billings in Figure 1-2). To meet the requirements of this problem we must identify the name of each industrial customer and record their average water use. We must also have columns showing water billings under current pricing and the new pricing for each customer. An additional column showing the change in the water bill for each customer can help us to quickly see which customers are benefitted and which are hurt by the new pricing. A total row is needed to indicate how alternative proposed rates will affect the amount billed to all industrial customers.

Identify and Describe Input Data Areas

After defining the appropriate row and column headings, we must determine where the data values for those rows and columns are to come from. The name of each industrial customer along with the customer's average monthly water use is to be obtained from existing records and entered onto the spreadsheet as input data. Thus we simply indicate an example of the data that will appear in each of these columns

Figure 1-2

A Sample Layout Form for the Western Water Company Application

```
┌─────────────────────────────────────────────────────────────────────┐
│                                                                     │
│        IMPACT OF PROPOSED RATE CHANGES ON INDUSTRIAL CUSTOMERS       │
│                                                                     │
│                                                                     │
│   BILLING PARAMETERS:      Existing              Proposed            │
│                             Rates                 Rates              │
│                                                                     │
│     Base Rate:               $.09                 $.99   ┐ Parameter │
│                                                          │ values to │
│     Gallon Cutoff for                                    │ be entered│
│       Tiered Rate:         100,000               999,999 ┤ repeatedly│
│                                                          │ by users  │
│     Tiered Rate:             $.07                 $.99   ┤ to evaluate│
│                                                          │ proposed  │
│                                                          │ rates     │
│   ESTIMATED BILLINGS:                                    ┘           │
│                                                                     │
│                  Average    Avg. Monthly Amount Billed   Change in   │
│     Customer     Monthly     Existing      Proposed      Amount      │
│       Name      Water Use     Rates         Rates        Billed      │
│    ┌──────────────────────┐ ┌─────────────────────────┐ ┌──────────┐│
│    │ Baxter Mining 182,755│ │ $999,999.99  $999,999.99│ │$999,999.99││
│    │    X(20)    9,999,999│ │ $999,999.99  $999,999.99│ │$999,999.99││
│    │                      │ │                         │ │          ││
│    │ (input data from paper│ │(computation:            │ │(computed ││
│    │  records of last year's│ │ if Water Use < Cutoff  │ │ values:  ││
│    │  customers and use)  │ │  Billing = Use x Base Rate│ │Proposed -││
│    │                      │ │ else Billing = Base Rate x│ │Existing ││
│    │                      │ │  Cutoff Volume + Tiered Rate│Amount  ││
│    │                      │ │  x (Water Use - Cutoff Vol))│Billed) ││
│    └──────────────────────┘ └─────────────────────────┘ └──────────┘│
│                             ┌──────────────────────────────────────┐│
│         TOTAL      9,999,999│ $999,999.99 (computed: sum of col above)│
│                             └──────────────────────────────────────┘│
└─────────────────────────────────────────────────────────────────────┘
```

NOTE: Once the spreadsheet has been developed and tested all cells except those containing the proposed rate parameters should be protected, and a backup copy of the spreadsheet should be maintained at all times.

Developing Spreadsheet Applications

and describe its source. In the example, layout form descriptions of the source of data are enclosed in parentheses. Examples of data can be shown via literal values (Baxter Mining 182,755). Generic examples of the format of columns of data may also be used. Where generic format descriptions are used, X represents any alpha character and 9 represents any numeric digit. Thus the X(20) under Customer Name suggests that the actual names will be up to 20 characters in length and will contain label (nonnumeric) values. Values for the next two columns must be computed based upon the Average Monthly Water Use for each customer and the prices charged per gallon. The rate structure parameters must appear on the layout form before the billing columns can be defined.

Identify and Describe Parameter Storing Cells

Information about the current and proposed pricing structure is a key element of the spreadsheet. Parameter values for the new pricing structure are to be adjusted repeatedly to evaluate their effects on billings and the parameters that are entered here apply to each individual customer. These parameter values should appear in a prominent place on the layout form. In Figure 1-2 we have defined a section of the report called billing parameters. We have three parameters in each rate structure: a base rate, a cutoff volume of gallons at which a tiered rate is to be applied, and the tiered rate to be applied to gallons of use beyond the cutoff volume. We must compute billings for both the existing rates and proposed rates. Literal values are shown under the existing rates column since these are historic and unchanging values. Dummy values are used to show the type of data to be recorded under the proposed rates, and the note to the right of the column describes how the data values are to be obtained.

Identify and Describe Areas Whose Values are to be Computed

With the billing parameters placed on the layout form, we return to the columns showing the amount billed for each customer under existing and proposed rates. A generic data type description is shown and then the calculation used to determine the data values for these columns is described. Here conditional (or if) logic is required. If a customer's gallons of water use is below the cutoff volume their bill is simply equal to their water use times the base rate per gallon. However, if their use exceeds the cutoff volume they are charged at the base rate for all gallons up to the cutoff volume and are charged at the tiered rate for the gallons beyond the cutoff volume. The final column in the Estimated Billings section is the Change in Amount Billed. As the description for this column on the layout form indicates, values for this column are calculated by simply subtracting the billing for a customer under the existing rates from the billing for that customer under the proposed rate. Finally, we must describe how the data values in the total row will be determined. As the description indicates, the column of individual customer data above, is simply summed to compute the total value for each column.

Notice that we were able to describe input, processing, and output requirements of this application in our layout form. The layout form indicates which portions of the spreadsheet will contain input data and where that data will come from. It also indicates portions of the spreadsheet that will display the results of processing operations and describes the processing required to produce those results. No areas of the layout form in Figure 1-2 are explicitly specified as output areas because, for this application, all of the information on the layout form is to be included in the output report. If only a portion of the contents of a layout form is to be included in a report or other output document, the layout form would indicate the boundaries of the output area. For example, if we were only interested in summary billing information, the billing information for individual customers could be moved to a different section or worksheet page within the spreadsheet. This section would not appear on the screen or be printed when the billing parameters and totals row are displayed or printed.

Add Descriptive Notes

Descriptive notes at the bottom of a layout form could be used to describe control measures that need to be imposed as the design is implemented. In our Western Water Company example formal control measures may not be needed if the spreadsheet is to be used only by its developer. However, suppose that the president of the company has only a very limited knowledge of how to use spreadsheets, but she wants to use the application herself to see the impact of different rate structures. Now it would become necessary to protect the application from accidental changes to formulas or fixed data values and to keep a clean backup copy of the application at all

Developing Spreadsheet Applications

times. The note at the bottom of the layout form in Figure 1-2 describes the control measures to be implemented.

The layout form we have just described may seem overly elaborate for such a simple application. Many experienced end users might sit down at a computer to create this sort of application with no more than a mental picture of its design. However, sketching a layout form for an application can lead to substantial reductions in development time and improvements in the appearance and functionality of the finished application. Tangible design documents, such as layout forms, become crucial for larger applications and it is good practice to sketch a layout form before sitting down at the computer to create an application of any size. For each case in this book you will either be given a layout form, or will be asked to develop one before coding the application.

CODING

Once analysis and design have been completed it is time to create the application in computerized form. This is done by typing in or coding the sets of data and instructions required to implement the application using an appropriate software package. The applications in this chapter are to be implemented using spreadsheet software.

As mentioned in the preface, this casebook is designed for use by students with at least some experience in the use of spreadsheets and database management software. The spreadsheet instructions required to implement applications will not be described here.

To test your familiarity with fundamental spreadsheet operations, you should build a spreadsheet file to implement the Western Water Company application that we have designed. You can compare your work to the spreadsheet file called **western** on your data disk. Two versions of this file are available, a LOTUS version stored as **western.wk3** and an EXCEL version stored as **western.xlw**. Most other common spreadsheet packages will read one or both of these files.

NOTE: FOR ALL CASES WHERE A SPREADSHEET FILE IS PROVIDED BOTH A LOTUS AND AN EXCEL VERSION IS AVAILABLE ON YOUR DATA DISK. THE LOTUS VERSIONS ALL HAVE THE **.WK3** FILE EXTENSION AND THE EXCEL VERSIONS HAVE THE **.XLS** EXTENSION.

TESTING METHODS

The most basic type of testing of applications involves simply checking the accuracy of the results produced. All of the computations in an application should be tested by performing manual calculations on a set of test data and comparing the results to those produced by the computer application. The test data used should include a sample of every type of combination of data values that must be handled by the application. In our example, water use levels both below and above the volume cutoff for tiered pricing need to be tested to ensure that the application calculates all billings correctly. The application should also be tested by changing key parameters and ensuring that appropriate changes occur in all of the cells that should be affected by those changes. For example, in the Western Water Company application an increase in the base rate parameter should cause an increase in the amount billed for every customer, while a change in the tiered rate should affect only customers whose water use is greater than the volume cutoff level.

In addition to testing for accuracy, applications should also be tested for clarity and user friendliness. Is the application understandable? Are key results highlighted appropriately? Is the application easy for its users to operate? These questions should be addressed in testing the application. As inaccuracies or limitations are discovered they are immediately corrected and the application is retested in an iterative fashion until the user or users of the application are satisfied with its performance.

DOCUMENTATION

When an application is completed and turned over to users, it is particularly important that the users be provided with a complete and understandable set of instructions or *documentation* which will allow them to operate the application. Documentation can be in the form of separate written procedures describing the workings of an application. However, it is possible to create spreadsheet applications

Developing Spreadsheet Applications

which are self-documenting. To do this, a documentation section of the spreadsheet is created which simply contains a set of label entries describing how the spreadsheet is to be used. Normally this section is placed at the upper left corner of the spreadsheet so that it will automatically appear on the screen when the spreadsheet is retrieved.

Figure 1-3 shows a documentation section that might be used with our Western Water Company example. The only independent information required by the user would be instructions on how to access Lotus and retrieve the application file. Once the application spreadsheet is accessed, the instructions shown should be sufficient to allow a novice spreadsheet user who is not familiar with the application to use it effectively.

This sort of documentation is necessary for any application that will be used by someone other than its builder and is also crucial for any applications that will be used repeatedly over a long period of time. Even the developer is likely to forget some of the details of an application when he or she begins to use it again after a lapse of several weeks or months. Thus each spreadsheet should have a documentation section which describes the purpose of the application, indicates who developed it and when, describes key assumptions used, and describes the steps needed to operate the application successfully.

DESIGNING SPREADSHEETS WITH MULTIPLE SECTIONS

Spreadsheets frequently contain multiple sections. This is true even in our simple example case. With the documentation section shown in Figure 1-3, the spreadsheet has two largely independent sections. The documentation information needs to appear on the screen when the user first accesses the spreadsheet, but once it has been read the user moves on to the working portion of the spreadsheet.

Windows based spreadsheet packages allow you to have multiple worksheet pages in a single spreadsheet file. When a spreadsheet has multiple independent sections they should be placed on separate worksheet pages. This is necessary because placing differently structured sets of information in overlapping rows or columns of a single worksheet page can cause problems. Suppose two different sections of the application occupy common rows on the same worksheet page. Now if we need to add a row to the middle of one of the sections, this addition creates an undesired blank row in the middle of the working section. Similar problems can occur if two sections of a spreadsheet share common columns. Adding or deleting a column in one section would have unintended effects on the other section. In addition, each column can have only one width setting, so the two sections would be forced to use a common width for their shared columns which is often undesirable. This problem is avoided when independent sections of a spreadsheet are placed on separate worksheet pages.

Figure 1-3

A Sample Documentation Section
for the Western Water Company Case

```
             A
  1  IMPACT OF PROPOSED RATE CHANGES ON INDUSTRIAL CUSTOMERS
  2
  3  Developed by: Joe Jones    Date Developed: September, 1993
  4
  5  This spreadsheet provides an analysis of the effect of changes in
  6  water rate structures on billings to industrial customers.
  7
  8  To begin using this spreadsheet, simply click on the worksheet tab
  9  labeled WESTERN at the lower left of your screen.
 10
 11  You may enter trial values for the Proposed Rates parameters in
 12  column E and their impact on billings will be automatically computed.
 13
 14  To get a printed listing of the results, simply click on the
 15  print icon. This will cause a report to be printed. As the report
 16  is printed, you will be returned to the entry mode. You can print
 17  reports for as many sets of rates as you want by simply repeating
 18  this process.
 19
 20  When you are finished using this spreadsheet, simply Exit from it
 21  without saving your changes. This will retain the spreadsheet
 22  in its original form for your next session.
 23
 24
 25  **********************************************************************
```

Developing Spreadsheet Applications

In larger applications, there may be several independent sections of the spreadsheet. For example, a spreadsheet application might have a documentation section, a section to store input data, a section for storing some intermediate computations, and sections for storing two independent sets of results for output reporting. Figure 1-4 shows how such an application should be laid out. Each section is placed on a separate worksheet page. The documentation section is placed on either the first or last worksheet page. In designing this type of application, the developer may create a separate layout form to describe the design of each of the major sections of the application.

If you are using a software package which does not allow you to use multiple worksheet pages in a single spreadsheet file, you can achieve the same effect by placing each section of your spreadsheet in a separate, nonoverlapping set of rows and columns. For example, the documentation section of Figure 1-4 might be placed in row A columns 1 through 25, the input section in columns B through H and rows 26 through 48, the scratch section in columns I through N and rows 49 through 74, and so on.

SUMMARY

The development process for end user applications has three main components. These are: analysis and design, coding, and testing and documentation.

The analysis of an application focuses on the requirements of that application with respect to: the output to be produced, the inputs available, the transformation process to be used, storage needs, and the controls that should be imposed. Based upon the requirements of the application, a determination is made about the type of software to be used in developing the application. The developer then proceeds to design a solution which will meet the requirements and can be implemented using the selected software.

Figure 1-4

Layout for a Multi-Section Spreadsheet

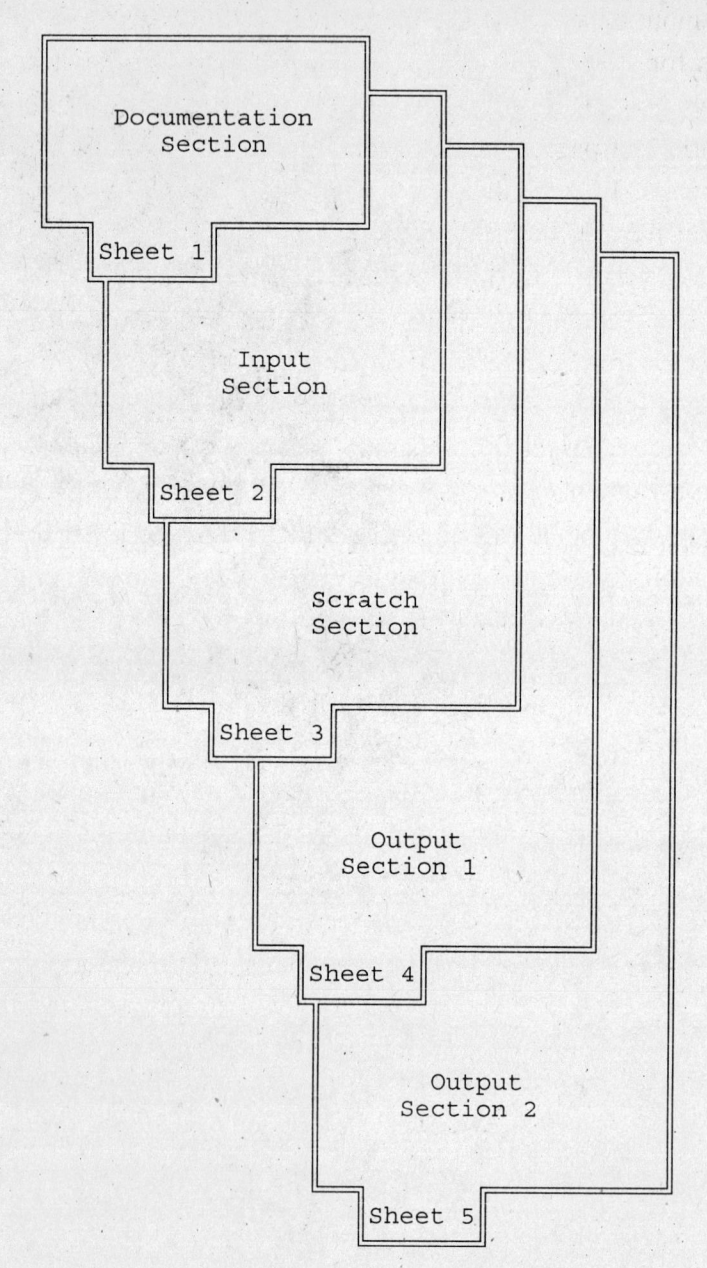

Documentation Section
Sheet 1

Input Section
Sheet 2

Scratch Section
Sheet 3

Output Section 1
Sheet 4

Output Section 2
Sheet 5

Developing Spreadsheet Applications

The layout form is a design tool which provides a visual representation of an application's design. Layout forms are most often used to document the output of applications. However, layout forms can be used to represent all components of most simple spreadsheet applications. For each spreadsheet case in this book you will either be given a layout form for the application or will be asked to create one before you implement the application on the computer.

Coding involves the generation of computer instructions to implement the application's design using the selected software package. The spreadsheet cases presented in this book can be implemented using any common spreadsheet software package.

Application testing involves both testing for the accuracy of processing performed by the application and testing for user friendliness. Hand calculations performed on test data are used to ensure the accuracy of an application. In addition, the user(s) of an application should test it to ensure that it is understandable to them and provides for their needs in an appropriate, user friendly fashion. Errors or inadequacies should be corrected as they are discovered so that coding and testing occurs in an iterative fashion until all users are satisfied with the application.

Documentation provides users with the information they need to use an application effectively. Most spreadsheet applications can be almost entirely self-documenting. We can make an application self-documenting by adding a documentation section. The documentation section describes the steps required to use the application effectively and also documents fundamental features of the application.

CHAPTER 2: SPREADSHEET CASES

CASE 1: Daydreams Day Care Centers

Daydreams Day Care Centers offer preschool (day care) services and a kindergarten program. Daydreams currently operates four day care centers, all of which are located in the city of Madisonville. Janet Adams founded Daydreams as a day care center operating in a single location in one of Madisonville's upper middle class neighborhoods. This initial center was quite successful. Janet soon found that she had reached the capacity of the building she was renting and was turning away applicants. It was time to expand her operations.

Janet knew that several parents were bringing their children from distant neighborhoods to her day care center. She had also received requests from a number of parents asking if she could recommend a day care center in their neighborhood with a philosophy similar to that of the Daydreams center. Therefore, Janet began to look for additional sites in residential neighborhoods throughout Madisonville. Over the past five years her operations have expanded to the current level of four centers.

As Daydreams has grown, Janet has kept operational decision-making as decentralized as possible. She continues to serve as the director of the original center and thus has little time available to manage operations at the other centers. Her philosophy has been to hire a creative and responsible director for each center and then give that director full responsibility for and control over operations within their center.

A budget is established for each center based on negotiations with its director. The rates charged to customers are designed to recover a target return based on the budgeted expenses. While this freedom has attracted creative directors and a loyal customer base, Janet has found that some of her directors have had poor budget discipline or simply have paid little attention to budgetary matters. There have been several occasions, in recent years, when a director has substantially overspent their budget. To limit similar problems in the future, Janet feels that she needs to have a better means of keeping track of performance against budget.

Record keeping at Daydreams is done in manual form. Janet Adams has used a local CPA firm to process her records for reporting and tax purposes, since the inception of her business. The reports they have produced have been effective for tax purposes and in securing financing. Janet does receive monthly reports showing expenditures by category in each center. However, these reports do not give Janet a way to quickly see when one of her centers may be in danger of significantly overspending its budget. What she would like to have is a set of summary information for each of her centers on a monthly basis showing expenses to date in each broad budget category and comparing those expenditures to budgeted levels in a meaningful way.

Knowing that you have experience in the use of spreadsheet packages, Janet asks you to try to develop a spreadsheet report that will give her the information she needs. She is able to give you a copy of the budget for each center and a set of year-to-date expenditure reports for the month just ended.

Janet indicates that expenditures in most of the budget categories tend to occur at a constant pace throughout the budget year. Some directors tend to buy most of their supplies on a once or twice a year basis. However, Janet feels that she can deal with these variations on a judgmental basis. She suggests that comparisons be based upon percentage of budget expended versus the percentage of the budget year that has passed.

She also indicates that, if your report provides the information she needs she would like you to produce it in updated form as each month's expenses become available. She would also plan to continue running the application in succeeding years with updated budget data. As a starting point for your analysis she gives you a set of budget data for the 1995-96 fiscal year and a set of year-to-date expenditures data for the most recent available month. This information is presented below and is available in a spreadsheet file named **daydata** on your data disk.

Spreadsheet Cases

Application Development Notes

A proposed structure for the spreadsheet and layout forms for the report portions of this application are presented in figures below. Where the layout form indicates *copy from the cell address* it means that the cell address containing this value should be used as a formula for the cell. This causes the value to be copied to the new cell and at the same time ensures that changes to the value stored in the input cell will automatically be reflected when the value is used in other parts of the spreadsheet. The proportion of the budget year that has expired serves as a parameter for this spreadsheet. The Pro-Rated Budget amounts shown are based on the assumption that expenditures should be evenly distributed over the budget year. Thus, if four months of the budget year have expired, 4/12 or one-third of the budget should have been expended.

Assignment

1. Based upon the application description and the sample design materials provided, develop a spreadsheet for the Daydreams Day Care Centers that will help Janet Adams evaluate each center's compliance with its budget. Your spreadsheet should have a reporting area providing the comparisons described above and should be designed to allow new year-to-date expenditures data to be quickly and effectively entered each month without risk of damaging the reporting area of the spreadsheet. Test your application for accuracy and completeness. Add a documentation section to make your spreadsheet as self documenting as possible.

2. Using a word processing package, write a memorandum to Janet Adams describing the procedures that you suggest she use in having your application updated each month. Incorporate copies of the output reports produced by your spreadsheet in this memorandum and add your assessment of what they indicate about the spending patterns of her day care centers.

DAYDREAMS DAY CARE CENTERS BUDGET - FISCAL YEAR 1995/96

Expenditure Category	Rush St.	Westside	Aspen Trail	Glen Valley
Wages and Salaries	164500	139825	200690	215824
Employee Benefits	30346	26609	39096	45643
Supplies	14625	11608	16507	21338
Equipment	4800	7250	3825	13240
Utilities	8450	6828	9693	9774
Rent	18000	14800	21000	22200
Insurance	12445	11300	13820	15640
Contract Services	8500	10500	10000	12400

Handwritten totals: 261666 228720 314631 356059

DAYDREAMS DAY CARE CENTERS YEAR-TO-DATE EXPENDITURES
July 1 - November 30, 1995

Expenditure Category	Rush St.	Westside	Aspen Trail	Glen Valley
Wages and Salaries	64673	60299	96579	90549
Employee Benefits	11930	11475	18814	19149
Supplies	5921	3957	7422	9774
Equipment	2352	2946	1864	6312
Utilities	3037	2601	3803	2590
Rent	7500	6166	8750	9250
Insurance	5185	4708	5758	6516
Contract Services	2786	4924	5527	5792

Handwritten ratios (Rush St.): 0.393, 0.393, 0.405, 0.49, 0.359, 0.417, 0.417, 0.328
Handwritten ratios (Westside): 0.431, 0.431, 0.341, 0.406, 0.381, 0.417, 0.417, 0.469
Handwritten ratios (Aspen Trail): 0.481, 0.481, 0.45, 0.487, 0.392, 0.417, 0.417, 0.55
Handwritten ratios (Glen Valley): 0.42, 0.42, 0.45, 0.48, 0.265, 0.417, 0.417, 0.467

Handwritten totals: 103584 97076 148517 149932

Spreadsheet Cases

Spreadsheet Components Diagram

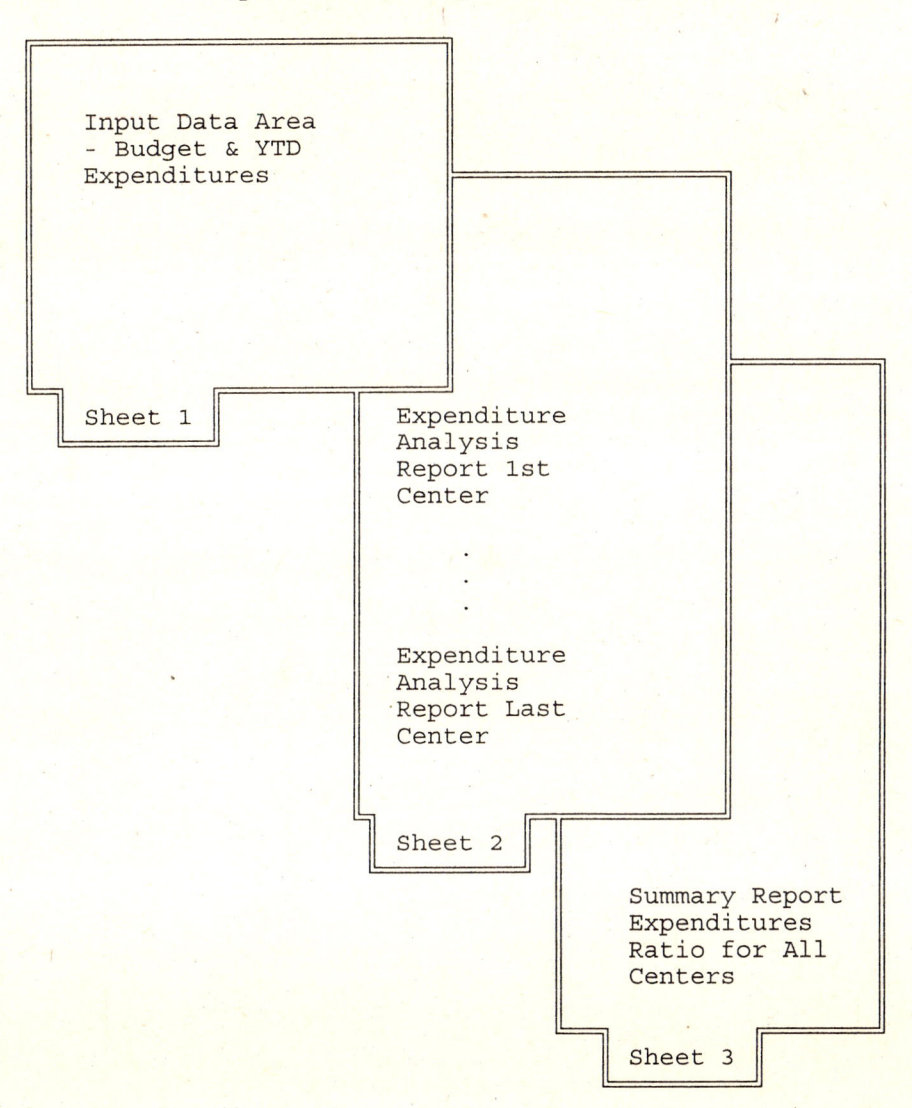

```
┌─────────────────────────┐
│                         │
│  Input Data Area        │
│  - Budget & YTD         │
│  Expenditures           │
│                         │
│                         │
│                         │
│           ┌─────────────┴───────┐
│           │                     │
│           │                     │
└───────────┤  Expenditure        │
  Sheet 1   │  Analysis           │
            │  Report 1st         │
            │  Center             │
            │                     │
            │        .            │
            │        .            │
            │        .            │
            │                     │
            │  Expenditure        │
            │  Analysis           │
            │  Report Last        │
            │  Center             │
            │                     │
            │         ┌───────────┴─────┐
            │         │                 │
            └─────────┤  Summary Report │
              Sheet 2 │  Expenditures   │
                      │  Ratio for All  │
                      │  Centers        │
                      │                 │
                      └─────────────────┘
                            Sheet 3
```

Layout Forms

INPUT DATA AREA

As shown in sample data and given in the provided data file - **daydata**.

EXPENDITURE ANALYSIS REPORTS AREA

Report Parameters:

Months of Budget Year Expired	99	input value = number of months expired in budget year
Percent of Budget Year Expired	999.9%	Months Expired / 12

Year-to-Date (YTD) Spending Versus Pro-Rated Budget
<u>(center name)</u> Center

Expenditure Category	(A) Year-to-Date Expenditures	(B) Pro-Rated Budget Allocation	(A) - (B) Expenditures Minus Budget	(A) / (B) Ratio Expenditures to Budget
Wages and Salaries Employee Benefits (copy from Expenditure Category column of input data area)	$999,999 (copy from cell addr. of corresponding cell in input data area)	$999,999 (corresponding cell from input data area * % of Budget Year Expired)	$999,999 (YTD Expenditures - Pro-Rated Budget)	9.99 (YTD Expenditures / Pro-Rated Budget)
TOTAL	(sum of column)			

SUMMARY EXPENDITURES RATIO REPORT

Ratio of Year-to-Date Expenditures to Pro-Rated Budget
<u>(report period e.g July-Oct., 1995</u>

Center

Expenditure Category	Rush St.	Westside	Aspen Trail	Glen Valley
Wages and Salaries Employee Benefits (copy from Expenditure Category column of input data area)	9.99	9.99	9.99	9.99
	(copy from cell address of corresponding cell for this ratio from the expenditure analysis reports area)			
TOTAL	.	.	.	.

Spreadsheet Cases

CASE 2: Bader Products

Bader Products is a mid-sized shoe manufacturing company. Bader has traditionally sold its shoes through retail shoe stores located in the central and western United States. Bader has a sales staff of 35 salespersons who are assigned to one of four regional sales managers. The regional managers in turn report to Alice Barnes the Vice President for Marketing. The sales staff at Bader products has always been assigned on a purely regional basis with each salesperson selling all product lines to customers within her or his territory.

Three years ago Bader introduced a new product line, the Thoot. A Thoot is a type of thong that can be comfortably worn while hiking or engaging in other strenuous activities. This new product line has proven to be quite successful, with sales reaching 12% of total company sales after three years. However, Alice believes that sales growth in this new product line has been hampered by the structure of Bader's sales staff.

The new product line is sold primarily through camping equipment retailers. Some members of the sales staff have been quick to recognize the need to seek out this new type of customer while others have not. Alice feels that the set of customers for the Thoots product line is sufficiently different to require a separate sales staff. She proposes to establish an initial sales force of four salespersons, one for each of Bader's sales regions. Each salesperson would then be responsible for selling Thoots throughout his or her entire region.

Alice feels that the current sales territories need to be restructured and that some territories can be consolidated. Alice has received approval from the CEO to make this move providing that she does not increase the total sales staff and that the salespersons for the new team are selected entirely from the existing sales staff.

Salespersons who are considered "good" candidates for the new sales team will be invited to apply. Alice has asked you to prepare a spreadsheet for her that will identify these "good" candidates. She feels that two characteristics are particularly important. First, the Thoots sales staff will have to seek out many new customers and thus the salespersons selected should have a history of seeking out new customers. Second, Thoots salespersons should be individuals who have been enthusiastic about selling this new line. Thus, the salespersons selected should have a strong track record in sales of Thoots. She also feels that the sales quota should be considered when evaluating the performance of the sales staff. The quotas are felt to be good measures of the sales potentials of different territories, and often new salespersons are given the least promising territories. She asks you to consider sales for the last two years in your analysis.

The information systems department was able to extract summary data from organizational databases and place it in spreadsheet format for you. This data is on your data disk in a file named **badrdata** and the first 10 rows of this spreadsheet are reproduced below. For each salesperson the following items have been retrieved. S_NAME - the salesperson's name, QUOTA94 - the sales quota for 1994 in $, NCUST94 - sales to new customers in 1994 in $, THOOTS94 - sales of Thoots in 1994 in $, QUOTA95 - the sales quota for 1995, NCUST95 - sales to new customers in 1995, and THOOTS95 - sales of Thoots in 1995.

Application Development Notes

A sample layout form for this application is shown below. Two work sections, or worksheet pages, are needed for this spreadsheet file. The input data should look like the sample data shown and this portion of the spreadsheet has been created for you. The second section of the application is a worksheet for the sales performance report that you are to create. The data used for this report is to come from the sum of sales over both 1994 and 1995. Thus, the values for cells displaying the dollar sales amounts must be found by adding the cell containing the 1994 amount to the cell containing the 1995 amount. There are multiple criteria to be used in evaluating sales performance. Thus both the rate of Sales to New Customers and the Rate of Sales of Thoots are presented. A last column called High Sales is added which is designed to identify salespersons who have shown strong performance on both criteria. Salespersons whose percentage sales in both of the target categories are more than 15 percent above average are to be identified as having high sales. Finally, in order to highlight the top candidates, the entire data area of the report is sorted from high to low based on Sales of Thoots as a percentage of Sales Quota.

Spreadsheet Cases

Assignment

1. Using the input data and layout forms provided, develop a spreadsheet application to provide Alice Barnes with information highlighting those salespersons who are good candidates to join the new sales team. Be sure to test your application for accuracy and completeness. Add a documentation section to your spreadsheet to make it as self documenting as possible.

2. Write a memorandum to Alice Barnes describing the results of your application. Incorporate a copy of your Sales Performance Report in your memorandum. Make preliminary recommendations to Ms. Barnes based upon this report. Also suggest to her any limitations you see in the analysis and any other factors which you would suggest she look at.

```
                    Sample of Input Sales Data
SALESP_NAME        QUOTA94   NCUST94   THOOTS94  QUOTA95   NCUST95   THOOTS95
Adams, Ann          619600     90421     80459    641200    136002    111897
Arnot, Bob          682100     98822     91867    703700    226163    178837
Bates, Judith       765100    136654     76267    774800    257321    174854
Bowles, Barbara     707300    127265    100064    712300    186979    136160
Choate, Dan         773200     89520     94315    805500    192234    146595
Davis, John         782600     40200     33217    816100    157040    142844
Dunn, Sally         819700    111444     76549    825800    169847    103110
Evans, Mindy        527600     87159     76144    533100    139653     87186
Files, Allan        648600     44667     38080    653200    195565    161372
Giles, Janet        772200    211339    142521    806600    118503    124575
```

Layout Forms

INPUT DATA AREA

As shown above and as defined in spreadsheet file **badrdata**.

SALES PERFORMANCE REPORTING AREA

	TOTAL DOLLAR AMOUNT OF			SALES IN CATEGORY AS A % OF SALES QUOTA		
Salesperson Name	Sales Quota	Sales to New Cust.	Sales of Thoots	Sales to New Cust.	Sales of Thoots	High Sales*
Xxxxx, Xxxxx Xxxxx, Xxxxx (copy from corresponding cell address in input data area)	$9,999,999 $9,999,999 (sum of 91 and 92 values for each variable from the input data area)	$999,999 $999,999	$999,999 $999,999	99.99% 99.99% (New Cust. Sales / Sales Quota)	99.99% 99.99% (Thoots Sales / Sales Quota)	Xxx Xxx
AVERAGE	(average of column above					

* A salesperson has "High Sales if both their sales rate to new customers and their sales rate of Thoots are more than 15 % above average.

(cell value = "Yes" if Sales of Thoots >= 1.15 * Average Sales of Thoots and Sales to New Customers >= 1.15 * Average Sales to New otherwise cell value is "   ".

NOTE - the entire data area for this report should be sorted in descending order on Sales of Thoots as a % of Sales Quota.

Spreadsheet Cases

CASE 3: Howard's Steak House

You have been hired to manage Howard's Steak House. Howard's has been in operation for 17 years. It was founded by Ralph and Susan Howard. The Howards managed the business themselves until Ralph's death nine years ago. Since that time Susan Howard has gradually reduced her involvement in operations. As she reduced her involvement in the business, she assigned part-time managerial duties to long time staff members.

Recently Susan Howard has become more and more concerned about how well her restaurant is being managed. She fears that some of the workers given managerial responsibilities have not had good management skills. She feels that she no longer has the time required to provide oversight and leadership to her restaurant operations. She has hired you to provide that oversight and leadership.

Howard's Steak House actually operates as two semi-independent operations. The bar at Howard's is called Susan's Skyline Bar. There is a separate manager for the bar and for the restaurant on each shift and financial statements are maintained separately for the bar operations and the restaurant operations.

Susan Howard has provided you with annual financial statements for Howard's Steak House and Susan's Skyline Bar for the past five years. You suggest that you would like to analyze these financial statements and observe operations for a couple of weeks. Then you would like to meet with her and the shift managers to begin to address any problems you see. To give yourself a better feel for the status of operations, you decide to create a spreadsheet that will evaluate the income statements for the past five years. You want your spreadsheet to highlight changes in revenue and cost components over time. You are preparing this application primarily for your own use. However, you plan to show printed results from this application to Susan Howard and the shift managers if they show important areas of concern that require their attention.

To facilitate comparisons across years you plan to produce a set of "common size" income statements. Common size income statements express various expense and revenue categories as percentages of total sales revenue. This facilitates comparisons of the distribution of revenue and expenses across time.

Because you are working with data that shows trends over time, you will want to create graphs summarizing the tabular results produced by your spreadsheet. Graphical results will help you to see trends more clearly and will probably be more meaningful to Susan Howard and her shift managers. You plan to create two sets of graphs one showing overall revenue and profitability trends in dollar terms, and another showing trends in the percentage distribution of expenses.

At the current time this is expected to be a one shot application. However, you are considering revising this application at some later date so that it can be updated and routinely run on an annual basis. You plan to produce printed reports and graphs from your spreadsheet for use by others, but you will be the only person serving as a direct user of the application.

The relevant income statement data for Howard's Steak House and Susan's Skyline Bar are shown below. To ensure that you understand these statements please note following facts about the information presented:

a. The Other Op. Expenses category is a general category for operating expenses not covered elsewhere. It includes items such as laundry expenses, miscellaneous supplies, and repair expenses.

b. The value of TOTAL OP. EXPENSES is equal to the sum of all of the expense categories above it.

c. The value of PRETAX INCOME is equal to SALES REVENUES minus TOTAL Op. Expenses.

d. Income Tax is calculated each year based on PRETAX income and the applicable tax rate which may vary from year to year.

e. The value of NET INCOME is equal to PRETAX INCOME minus Income Taxes.

Spreadsheet Cases

SUMMARY INCOME STATEMENT DATA FOR YEARS 1991-1995

Howard's Steak House

	Year				
	1991	1992	1993	1994	1995
SALES REVENUES	513258	550982	598991	609473	628945
OPERATING EXPENSES					
Food Costs	216235	230436	263627	265353	268179
Wages / Employee Benefits	165063	184521	215504	219288	230008
Rent	30000	30000	31200	31200	31200
Depreciation	12255	11820	10980	15250	14690
Other Op. Expenses	21608	21598	24841	20199	23353
TOTAL OP. EXPENSES	445161	478375	546152	551290	567430
PRETAX INCOME	68097	72607	52839	58183	61515
Income Taxes	23152	24686	16908	18618	19684
NET INCOME	44945	47921	35931	39565	41831

Susan's Skyline Bar

	Year				
	1991	1992	1993	1994	1995
SALES REVENUES	319811	331370	348960	363464	389220
OPERATING EXPENSES					
Beverage Costs	109141	112471	127514	141485	160852
Wages / Employee Benefits	100182	101736	109164	108106	122522
Rent	15000	15000	15600	15600	15600
Depreciation	7525	7080	6620	7826	7340
Other Op. Expenses	7542	7862	7502	7537	7170
TOTAL OP. EXPENSES	239390	244149	266400	280554	313484
PRETAX INCOME	80421	87221	82560	82910	75736
Income Taxes	27343	29655	26419	26531	24235
NET INCOME	53078	57566	56141	56379	51501

Application Development Notes

A sample layout form for this application is shown below. Two spreadsheet areas and a set of spreadsheet graphs are needed. The input data area has already been described and is available to you in a spreadsheet file called **howdata** on your data disk. The second area of the spreadsheet is the common size reporting area which you are to create. As indicated, common size percentages are to be shown for each of the operating expense categories for each year. The common size value for an expense category is simply expenses in that category divided by sales revenue for the corresponding year.

Multiple graphs are to be produced for this spreadsheet, so you should name and save each graph as it is created. Layouts for graphs to be produced are also shown below. Data ranges to be graphed are varied, but always represent measures of one or more variable(s) over time. Thus, the set of years is the X axis variable for each of the graphs. The graph layouts shown represent only one of many acceptable ways of displaying the requested information.

Assignment

1. Using the sample data and layout forms provided, develop a spreadsheet application which will provide analysis of trends in the financial statements of Howard's Steak House and Susan's Skyline Bar over the past five years. Your spreadsheet should provide both reports and graphs as described in the layout forms. Be sure to test your application for completeness and accuracy. Add a documentation section to make your application self documenting.

2. Write a memorandum to Susan Howard describing your findings. Incorporate any reports and/or graphs needed to highlight your main findings. Based on these results describe any potential problem areas you have identified.

Spreadsheet Cases

Layout Forms

INPUT DATA AREA

As shown above and as defined in spreadsheet file **howdata**.

COMMON SIZE REPORTING AREA

    COMMON SIZE INCOME STATEMENT DATA FOR YEARS 1991-1995

Howard's Steak House

```
                Year
                1991      1992      1993      1994      1995

OPERATING EXPENSES
   Food Costs            99.9%     99.9%     99.9%     99.9%     99.9%
   Wages / Employee
      Benefits          (expenses for this category this year /
   Rent                  sales revenues for the corresponding
   Depreciation          year)
   Other Op. Expenses
TOTAL OP. EXPENSES
```

Susan's Skyline Bar

```
                Year
                1991      1992      1993      1994      1995

OPERATING EXPENSES
   Beverage Costs        99.9%     99.9%     99.9%     99.9%     99.9%
   Wages / Employee
      Benefits          (expenses for this category this year /
   Rent                  sales revenues for the corresponding
   Depreciation          year)
   Other Op. Expenses
TOTAL OP. EXPENSES
```

GRAPH LAYOUTS

   (Each to be produced for both Howard's Steak House
      and Susan's Skyline Bar)

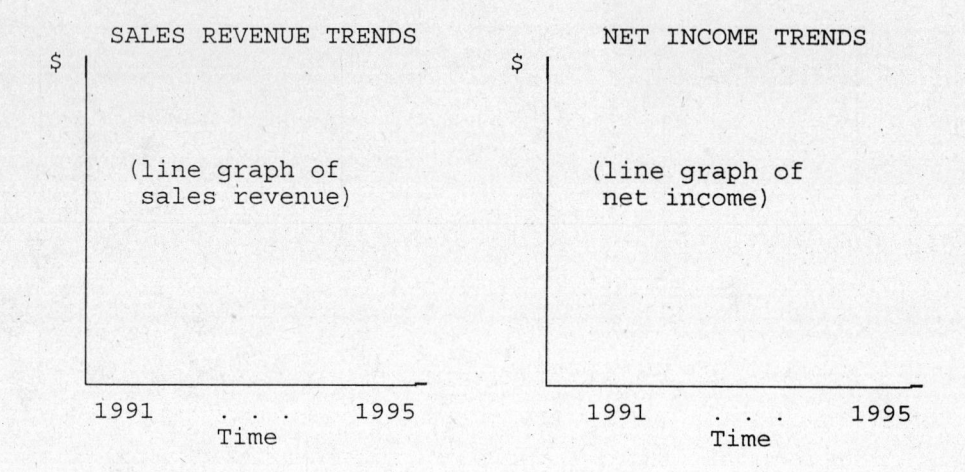

           SALES REVENUE TRENDS   NET INCOME TRENDS
      $| $|
       | |
       | |
       | (line graph of | (line graph of
       | sales revenue) | net income)
       | |
       | |
       | |
       |_____ |_____
         1991   . . . 1995   1991   . . . 1995
              Time   Time

                         OPERATING EXPENSE TRENDS

    % of Sales |
               |
               |
               |
               | (bar or stacked bar graph of
               | common size expenditures
               | for each of the operating
               | expenses categories)
               |
               |
               |
               |
               |_____
                 1991   1992   1993   1994   1995
                                   Year

CASE 4: Hot Pepper Mexican Restaurant

Maria Lopez has worked in restaurants for over 20 years. During that time she has worked as a waitress and cook and, more recently, as manager of a local restaurant. When the ownership of that restaurant changed. Maria decided to resign as manager and establish her own restaurant. Maria is recognized as an excellent cook of Mexican foods and she has many family recipes which will, she feels, be very popular with customers. Maria is planning to open her restaurant in a midwestern town of about 20,000 residents. Except for a fast food chain, there has not been a restaurant specializing in Mexican food in this town in several years.

Maria set out to develop the information needed to project revenues, expenses, and net income for her restaurant for the first five years of operation. Based on her long experience in the restaurant business, Maria has been able to develop rather precise estimates of her operating expenses. She has also developed estimates of expected revenues, although she feels that her revenue estimates are much more judgmental and subject to error. The information that Maria has been able to collect about her expected costs and revenues is summarized below.

Since her operations will involve a variety of different items selling at different prices, Maria has estimated the variable costs of operation as percentages of sales revenue. Maria's estimates of these costs are as follows:

```
Food and Beverage Costs:   33%
Labor Costs:               20%
Expendable Supplies:        3%
Miscellaneous:              6%
```

As variable cost elements change over time, Maria expects to make pricing adjustments that will keep the costs relatively stable in percentage terms. Thus, she estimates that the variable cost percentages shown will remain constant over the five year period.

In addition to these costs. Maria will face costs for the building and equipment for her restaurant and for utilities. maria views these as fixed costs. She does not plan to purchase either the building or the equipment. She will lease a restaurant site and rent the needed equipment based on annual lease and rental agreements. She has identified two potential sites for her restaurant. One is on Main Street and the other is on River Road. The Main Street site is more expensive, but it is also a more central location which is likely to attract more business. Maria anticipates that the same amount of equipment will be needed at either location and that utilities costs will be about the same at either location. She expects the equipment rental cost and the lease cost for either building to remain constant over the five year period. However, utilities costs are expected to increase by 7% per year. Her estimates of the annual costs for the building, equipment, and utilities are as follows:

```
Site Lease:
    Main Street site:         $30,000
    River Road site:          $18,000
Equipment Rental:             $13,200
Utilities:                    $ 7,500    + 7% per year
                                           increase
```

Maria also has developed estimates of projected sales levels. She expects that she should be able to have sales of $300,000 at the Main Street site by the second year of operation. Because the River Road site is more remote, she would expect only $250,000 in sales by the second year at that site. Maria also has some definite ideas about how the level of sales will change over time. Her experience has shown that sales for a new restaurant in its first year are typically only about 75% of the level achieved in the second year. After the second year, she expects sales to grow at about 5% per year as long as the restaurant remains successful. Her revenue estimates can be summarized as follows:

```
Base Sales Level (2nd year Sales):
    Main Street site:         $300,000
    River Road site:          $250,000
First year sales percentage:               75%
    (% of base sales level)
Growth rate for 3rd and
    succeeding Years                        5%
```

Spreadsheet Cases

Maria would like you to create a spreadsheet based on the estimates above. She wants this spreadsheet to provide projections of sales revenues, costs by category, and net pretax income for each of the first five years. She also wants these projections to be presented for each of the two potential restaurant sites for comparative purposes. Because many of the estimates she has given you are subject to uncertainty or error, she would like to be able to interact with the finished spreadsheet herself to see the impact of changes in any of the estimates she has made.

Net pretax income is equal to sales revenue minus total cost. Total cost is equal to total fixed cost plus total variable cost. All of the other formulas to be used in generating the needed projections have been described above.

Application Development Notes

A proposed set of layout forms for this application is presented below. The spreadsheet will have a parameters section and a projections reporting section. Since there is very little input data for this case, no data file is provided. All of the estimates provided in the discussion above are really parameters that are used to generate the projected values in the reporting section. To allow maximum flexibility for what-if analysis, each parameter must be fully described in the parameters section and its value must be entered just one time in the appropriate cell of the parameters section. All uses of a parameter in the calculations of the reporting section should reference the cell address where the parameter is stored. In fact, all formulas in the projections reporting area should only contain computations based on cell references - references to cells in the parameters area and/or references to other cells in the projections area. No formulas should contain numeric literal values. It is very important to test your spreadsheet by changing each of the parameter values and checking to ensure that appropriate changes occur in the projections area. Once your spreadsheet has been completed and tested, the areas containing formulas should be protected from accidental damage. Only the cells containing parameter values should be left unprotected for Maria's use.

Assignment

1. Based upon the application description and sample design materials provided, develop a spreadsheet for the Hot Pepper Restaurant that will help Maria Lopez evaluate the revenue prospects of each potential site. Your spreadsheet should have parameter and reporting areas as described above, and should allow Maria to change selected parameters and see their impact on the projections. Test your application for accuracy and completeness. Add appropriate controls to allow Maria to use the spreadsheet with minimal risk of loss or Damage. Add a documentation section to make your spreadsheet as self-documenting as possible.

2. Write a memorandum to Maria Lopez and attach a disk containing a copy of the spreadsheet file you created for her. Also include a printed copy of the set of projections for the base parameters she supplied and projections generated by at least two other sets of parameter values. Your memorandum should highlight key findings and should include a detailed description of procedures Maria will need to follow to use this application.

Layout Forms

PARAMETERS AREA (Numeric values shown are literal parameter values)

Cost and Revenue Parameters for the Hot Pepper Restaurant

```
    Variable Costs (expressed as a
      % of Sales Revenue):              Fixed Costs (Annual $ Amount):

    Food and Beverage Costs:    33%       Building Lease:
    Labor Costs:                20%         Main Street Site:       $30,000
    Expendable Supplies:         3%         River Road Site:        $18,000
    Miscellaneous:               6%       Equipment Rental:         $13,200
                                          Utilities (1st Year):    $ 7,500
                                            Ann. % increase in
                                            Utilities cost:              7%
    Sales Revenue:

       Base Sales Level (projected       Adjustments from Base Level
         second year sales):               for Sales in other Years:

         Main Street Site:   $300,000      1st Year sales as a %
         River Road Site:    $250,000        of Base Sales Level:        75%
                                           Sales Growth rate for
                                             3rd Year and beyond:         5%
```

Spreadsheet Cases

INCOME PROJECTIONS AREA

Projected Income from First Five Years of Operation

Main Street Site:

	Year 1	2	3	4	5
Sales Revenue:	1st Yr. Sales % * Yr. 2 Value	Base Sales Level	(1 + Sales growth rate) * prior year's value		

Variable costs:
  Food & Bev.
  Labor
  Supplies
  Miscellaneous
	percentage parameter for this cost element * Sales Revenue for this year				

TOTAL	sum of above 4 items				
Fixed Costs:					
Building	Lease parameter for this site				
Equipment	Equipment Rental Parameter				
Utilities	Utilities parameter	(1 + Utilities cost growth rate) * Prior year's value			
TOTAL	sum of above 3 items				
TOTAL COSTS	sum of Variable and Fixed Cost totals				
NET INCOME: (pretax)	Sales Revenue Minus Total Costs				

River Road Site:

. . . . . .
.
.   Projections for this site are based on the same formulas
.   as the main street site except that the Base Sales
    Level and Lease cost for the building are based on
    different parameter values.

> NOTE: The sizes of several rows and columns in the projections area were distorted to allow room for the entry of descriptions for the formulas to be used.

CASE 5: Currier Cams

Alan Blackbridge is foreman of the Cam Assembly Department at Currier Company. His department assembles a standard cam which is used as a component in a number of Currier products. Employees in Alan's department are paid an hourly amount plus 7 cents per unit produced. The Cam Assembly Department operates 3 shifts 5 days a week, and employs 8 production workers on each shift.

An inspector randomly inspects 50 units produced by each employee each night and records the number of defective units found. The inspector also records the number of hours worked and the total number of units produced by each employee at the end of each shift. The inspector for each shift turns in a Daily Production Slip.

At the end of each week Alicia Adams, Alan's secretary, must tabulate the total number of units produced by each employee and the number of defective units that were found. These weekly totals are recorded on a Hours and Production Report which must be sent to the Accounting department the accounting department converts this weekly data into computerized form and uses it to process payroll and to produce management reports, such as, the Production Trends Report which is sent to each department's foreman on a weekly basis. Samples of the Daily Production Slip, the Hours and Production Report, and a Production Trends Report are shown below.

Alan has become concerned by a decline in the productivity of his department over the last several weeks. Alan's own observation and conversation with shift supervisors have lead him to suspect that there may be problems of absenteeism and low productivity on certain shifts on certain days of the week. He also feels that the posting of summaries of the productivity of each shift on a weekly basis might generate a healthy competition between the shifts which could improve morale and output.

A personal computer has been installed in Alan's office He has acquired an introductory level of knowledge in the use of a popular spreadsheet package. His secretary Alicia has learned enough about this spreadsheet package to key in data, but has very limited knowledge of how to manipulate spreadsheets.

Spreadsheet Cases

Sample Documents from Currier Company Cams Department

Daily Production Slip

```
Inspector:
Shift:
Date:

| Employee | Emp. | Hours  | Units     | Rejected |
| Name     | Id#  | Worked | Assembled | Units    |
|          |      |        |           |          |
|          |      |        |           |          |
|          |      |        |           |          |
```

```
        Hours and Production Report
Department:         Cam Assembly
Week of (Monday):  10/07/96

Employee    Emp.   Hours    Units       Rejected
Name        Id#    Worked   Assembled   Units

J. Adams    2425   40.0     5637        17
A. Jones    3196   34.5     4732        13
B. Davis    4361   40.0     5391        11
   .          .      .         .          .
   .          .      .         .          .
```

```
    Production Trends Report       Week of:
    Cam Assembly Department        10/07/96

                    Average              Latest Week as % of
         Latest   Last 4    Year         Last 4      Year to
         Week     Weeks     to Date      Weeks Avg.  Date Avg

Units
Assembled: 611322  623593   642805        98.0%       95.1%

% of Units
Rejected:  4.7%    4.6%     4.1%         102.2%      113.3%
```

Alan believes that he needs an application that will do the following things:

1. record production information for each individual worker on a daily basis,

2. produce a summary report which can be used to compare performance across shifts and days of the week on a weekly basis.

3. automatically total the production information for each employee at week's end and produce the Hours and Production Report that must be sent to the accounting department.

Alan has asked you to design and develop this spreadsheet application for him. If you are successful, he plans to use this spreadsheet every week. He will have Alicia input the daily production data, while Alan himself plans to print out the weekly reports.

Application Development Notes

A sample of the set of data covering the most recently completed week is shown below. The full set of data for this week are available on the spreadsheet file called **curdata** on your data disk. Also shown below are: a diagram of the major components of this spreadsheet and layout forms for each component. Note that there are three components: an input data worksheet page, a section or worksheet page for the shift comparison reports to be used by Alan, and a worksheet page for the weekly hours and production report which is to be sent to the accounts receivable department. Many of the summary data values in the last two worksheet pages are obtained by summing appropriate cell ranges from the input data worksheet page, as described in the layout forms. This structure causes the last two areas to be automatically updated if new data are entered on the input data worksheet page.

Assignment

1. Using the input data and layout forms provided, develop a spreadsheet application to meet Alan Blackbridge's requirements as described above. Be sure to test your application for accuracy and completeness. Be sure that your

Spreadsheet Cases

application has appropriate controls to protect against accidental destruction of key formulas. Add a documentation section to your spreadsheet to make it as self documenting as possible.

2. Write a memorandum to Alan Blackbridge. In it describe your application and provide a detailed discussion of back-up and control procedures that should be used with this application.

```
                Sample Hours and Production Input data

                           Monday                   Tuesday
Employee   Emp.  Hours   Units   Reject  Hours   Units   Reject
Name       ID#   Worked  Prod.   Units   Worked  Prod.   Units      . . .

Day Shift

J. Adams   2425    8     1053      7       8     1126      4        . . .
A. Jones   3196    8      964      4       8     1148      3        . . .
B. Davis   4361    8      968      3       8     1077      1        . . .
C. Evans   4722    8     1017      5       8     1175      4        . . .
T. Date    5314    8     1019      2       8     1113      4        . . .
R. Rand    5408    8     1054      0       8     1160      4        . . .
L. Baker   6815    8     1045      3       8     1057      5        . . .
V. Lewis   7312    8     1073      3       8     1066      0        . . .

Evening Shift

B. Burt    1732    8     1134      2       8     1090      4        . . .
J. Bates   2073    8     1127      0       8     1110      2        . . .
     .       .     .       .       .       .       .       .
```

Spreadsheet Components for the Currier Cams Application

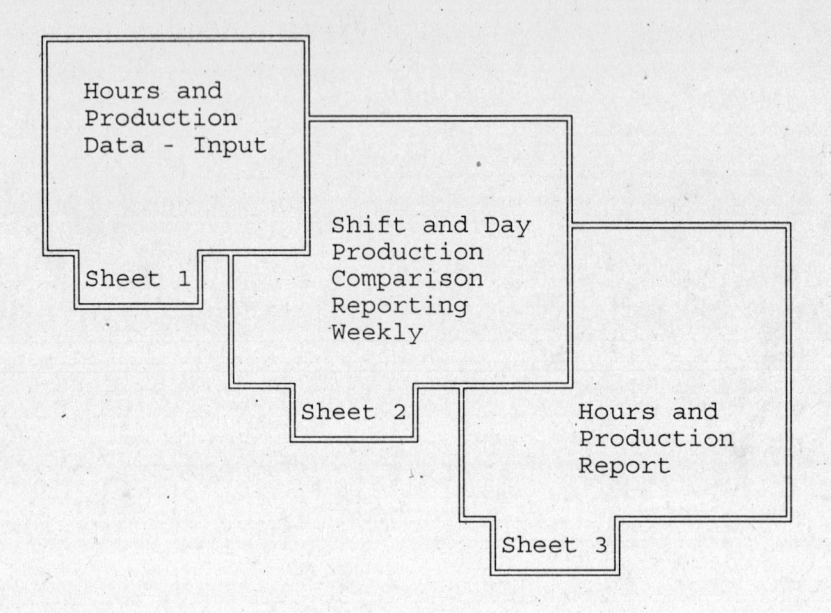

```
┌─────────────────┐
│ Hours and       │
│ Production      │
│ Data - Input    │
│        ┌────────┴────────┐
│        │ Shift and Day   │
│        │ Production      │
│ Sheet 1│ Comparison      │
└────────┤ Reporting       │
         │ Weekly          │
         │        ┌────────┴────────┐
         │        │ Hours and       │
         │ Sheet 2│ Production      │
         └────────┤ Report          │
                  │                 │
                  │         Sheet 3 │
                  └─────────────────┘
```

Currier Cams Layout Forms

A.   Daily Hours and Production Data

                         Monday   Tuesday . . . Friday

Employee Emp.   Hours   Units   Reject   . . .   Reject
  Name   ID#   Worked   Produced Units   Units

Day Shift

XXXXXXX 9999	99.9 9999 999 . . . 999
XXXXXXx 9999	99.9 9999 999 . . . 999
.	. . . . .
(names & ID#s	
input on	(Data input daily from Daily Production Slips)
initial spec-	
ification)	

Evening Shift

| . . . | .   .   . |

Night Shift

| . . . | .   .   . |

Spreadsheet Cases

Currier Cams Layout Forms (Continued)

B. Summary Shift and Day Comparison Report

```
                 Mon.    Tue.    Wed.    Thur.    Fri.  Week-to-date
```

Units Produced

Day Shift Evening Shift Night Shift	99999 99999 99999 99999 99999 (sum of units produced by shift on day from cells in the input data area)	99999 (sum of daily shift tots.)
Average	(average across the three shifts)	

% of Average Units Produced

Day Shift Evening Shift Night Shift	999.9% 999.9% . . . 999.9% (shift value divided by average) . . . . . .

Reject Units

Day Shift Evening Shift Night Shift	999 999 999 999 999 (sum of reject units by shift on day from cells in the input data area)	9999 (sum of daily shift tots.)
Average	(average across the three shifts)	

% of Average Reject Units

Day Shift Evening Shift Night Shift	999.9% 999.9% . . . 999.9% (shift value divided by average) . . . . . .

C. Weekly Hours and Production by Worker

```
Employee    Emp.         Hours      Units      Reject
  Name      ID#          Worked     Produced   Units
```

XXXXXXX 9999 XXXXXXX 9999 . (names and ID#s copied from input area above) XXXXXXX 9999	99.9 99999 999 99.9 99999 999 (sum of category over days of the week for each worker from cells in the input data area) 99.9 99999 999

43

CASE 6: Point Landes City Government

Like many cities, the City of Point Landes has experienced budget problems for several years. Pay raises to employees have averaged less than the increase in the cost of living and in some years salary levels have been frozen. Staffing levels have been cut to the point where it is felt that further reductions in staffing cannot be made without seriously reducing the level of services provided. The city budget remains tight and there is little prospect of gaining approval of tax increases to augment the budget.

The city's budget problems have been compounded by the fact that certain categories of personnel related expenditures, most notably health insurance costs, have been increasing in an uncontrollable fashion. The city has always paid all of the costs of health insurance for its employees and their dependents. The cost of health insurance has risen sharply for each of the past five years and the city's insurance carrier is raising its rates another 12 percent for the upcoming year.

Point Landes Personnel Director Dan Bates investigated several other potential insurance carriers when he received word of the rate increase. He was unable to find a better rate for comparable coverage. He next spoke with the city's current insurer about alternatives. They were able to propose a revised policy which would raise some deductibles and limit some coverages. This revised policy would cost 6 percent less than the current cost of the existing coverage (18 percent less than the cost of existing coverage for the upcoming year). However, this would represent a reduction in the level of benefits provided to city employees. The city has never reduced benefit levels in the past.

Preliminary budget meetings have been held with city manager Ann Evans to develop a proposed budget for the new fiscal year. The city manager has reluctantly agreed that the city will fully fund the increased health insurance costs. However, given the poor revenue outlook for the coming fiscal year, she is only willing to do this if the salaries are frozen for the year. If employees are willing to accept the modified health insurance coverage package, she is willing to grant a raise equivalent to the amount of cost savings that this reduction in coverage will generate.

Spreadsheet Cases

An employee relations committee was created four years ago. This committee gives employees a chance to be involved in budget and policy decisions. It was hoped that allowing employee input to these decisions would limit the threat of work slowdowns or stoppages. The proposed salary and benefits package for the coming year are to be presented to this committee. Dan Bates anticipates that his meeting with the employee relations committee will be a difficult one. If committee members are to be "won over" to acceptance of the budget constraints for the next year, they must become convinced of the severity of the impact of rising employee benefit costs on the city's budget. Only then will Dan be able to focus attention on the available choices.

Dan wants to be able to present summary information to the employee relations committee showing how the city's personnel costs have changed over the last five years. He has several ideas about how the data should be presented. As far as possible, he wants data to be expressed on a per employee basis. This gives committee members a better feel for the magnitudes involved. He wants the data to be organized in a way that highlights the impact of increases in employee benefit costs over time. He suggests that a five year historical period should be used. He wants the information to be conveyed graphically when possible. However, he wants the information that is presented graphically to be backed up by printed summary tables. Experience has taught him that some committee members are skeptical of graphical presentations and question "where the numbers came from."

Dan has asked you to prepare a set of spreadsheet reports and graphs highlighting the information he has described to you. You have been able to secure the set of data shown below from historic budget and personnel files.

PERSONNEL EXPENSES (in $1,000)

Expense Category	Year 1991	1992	1993	1994	1995
Wages and Salaries	4,682	4,604	4,535	4,735	4,803
Health Insurance	412	440	503	542	1,187
Retirement*	503	517	519	523	527
Other Benefits	172	174	175	177	177

*Employer Contributions to Retirement Funds

EMPLOYMENT LEVEL

```
         Average
         Number of
   Year  Employees
   1991      207
   1992      199
   1993      196
   1994      197
   1995      195
```

Application Development Notes

Since the amount of data used in this case is quite small, no input data file is created for you. You will want to create appropriate labels and enter the data shown in the tables above. You will want to create an area showing expenditures on a per employee basis, and time trends for those per employee expenditures. You should also create several appropriate graphs. Since more than one graph is needed, name and save each graph as you create it. In general, line or bar graphs are good for showing trends. Pie charts can be very effective for showing the relative size of components of something.

Assignment

1. Based on the descriptions and data above, design a layout form or set of layout forms for this application. Develop a spreadsheet to implement your design. Be sure to test your application for accuracy and completeness. Add a documentation section to your spreadsheet to make it as self-documenting as possible.

2. Write a memorandum to Dan Bates to accompany copies of the key reports and graphs produced by your application. In this memorandum, summarize major features and areas of concern that you see in the results.

CASE 7: Datius Software Corporation

The Datius Software Corporation is a medium sized software development company located in the "Silicon Valley" area of northern California. Turnover is a serious problem for all computer technology firms in this area and for Datius in particular. The projects which Datius undertakes require coordinated efforts of project development teams which work together for as long as three years on a large scale project. Work is seriously disrupted when employee turnover occurs. New employees not only must be brought up to speed on the technical details of a project, but they must also develop working and social relationships with other team members.

Susan Santee, the Personnel Director at Datius, feels that programs encouraging employee interaction outside the work environment can help to address both aspects of this problem. Such programs can help to strengthen social relationships between employees and help to build those relationships more quickly. The increased camaraderie created should also improve overall morale and reduce employee turnover.

One program that has come to Susan's attention is the offering of free or reduced-rate health club memberships to employees. Such a program would be offered through a health club facility very near the Datius office complex. This would make it easy for Datius employees to use health club facilities before or after work, or even during the lunch hour. By promoting use of health club facilities around the time and place of work, it is felt that employees will schedule activities together or simply "run in to each other" in the health club facility. Another consideration in Susan's mind is the fact that several competing software development firms have begun offering this "perk" to their employees. Susan feels that it is time to investigate the costs of such a program.

She begins her investigation by examining the types of health club membership options offered by related firms in the area. She discovers that some larger firms have their own "in plant" facilities. Many firms do not offer health club services at all. The remainder offer free or reduced price memberships to a health club with at least one facility within the immediate area of their offices. When memberships are offered, married employees are normally given family memberships. She decides to investigate the costs of fully supporting memberships for all employees, including family memberships, if desired, for married employees.

At this point she begins discussions with health clubs. She is able to find three health clubs with nearby facilities which are willing to offer a corporate membership for Datius employees.

1. HealthyBodz operates a single facility which is located two blocks from the Datius offices. It offers a full range of health club services, although the number of racquetball courts appears limited. The owner is willing to guarantee that new courts will be built if Datius signs a contract with his club.

    HealthyBodz owner quotes you a flat rate of $21 per membership per month. For this fee single employees could receive a membership and all married employees could receive a family membership. They would charge Datius only for those employees requesting membership cards from the club.

2. The Sweat Shop operates from a single, large-scale, facility which is located approximately 4 blocks from the Datius offices. It offers a full range of services and appears to have sufficient facilities to accommodate the needs of all Datius employees without further expansion.

    The ownership of the Sweat Shop quotes you a price of $12.50 for each single employee and $17.50 for each married employee per month. For this fee every employee would receive a membership and all married employees would receive a family membership. This rate is offered with the understanding that cards will be issued to all employees.

3. The Health Racket operates five health club facilities in the greater metropolitan area. The nearest facility is approximately one-quarter mile from the Datius offices. This facility currently offers only a limited number of aerobics classes, but all other facilities and services appear to be more than adequate. The ownership of The Health Racket is willing to commit to offering additional aerobics classes as needed if Datius signs a contract with them.

Spreadsheet Cases

The ownership of The Health Racket quotes you a price of $18 per individual membership and $24 per family membership per month. They would charge Datius only for those employees requesting membership cards from the club.

In order to compare this alternative to the others Susan sees that she will need to have a reasonable estimate of the proportion of employees who would plan to attend the club and become members. To assess the third plan, Susan also needs to know how many married employees will sign up for family memberships, and how many will sign up for individual memberships. Married employees might opt for individual memberships if they have a family membership in a club near their home, for instance. She has her secretary do a quick phone survey to estimate the interest level. The secretary is to randomly select about 25 employees from each of four demographic categories for the survey. The survey categories and results are shown below. Employees are split into age categories of 35 or under and over 35 because Susan feels that younger employees are more likely to want to join a health club. For married employees, the employee is asked whether they would request a family membership or just an individual membership.

```
TELEPHONE SURVEY RESULTS
                                   Number Who Would Request
Marital                Number       An Individual    A Family
Status     Age         Surveyed     Membership       Membership

Single    35 or <        26             23               -
Single     > 35          22             13               -
Married   35 or <        27              8              16
Married    > 35          25              3              15
```

To generate estimates of the costs of the alternatives the employment levels for these demographic groups are also needed. From personnel records in a database Susan was able to retrieve the following data about the current level of employment in each demographic group used in the survey:

Marital Status	Age	Number of Employees
Single	35 or <	178
Single	> 35	59
Married	35 or <	142
Married	> 35	169

Susan asks you to develop a spreadsheet for her that will produce estimates of the total monthly cost of each of the three programs based on the survey and employment data provided above. Susan indicates to you that she feels that the prices quoted by the health clubs are negotiable. However, she feels that each club will stick with their current rate structures. For instance, the Sweat Shop might drop their rates to $11.50 for single memberships and $16.00 for family memberships, but they would continue to insist on issuing memberships to all employees and charging for all employees. Susan wants you to create a spreadsheet that will allow her to easily enter changes in rates that she might be able to negotiate and immediately see their impact on the costs of a plan.

Application Development Notes

Because the amount of input data to be processed is small no input data file is provided. You will need to enter the survey and employment level data and use it to provide data that can be applied to the sets of rates offered by the three health clubs. To estimate the number of employees in each demographic group who will participate in the health club, calculate the percentage of participation based on the survey and multiply that by the number of employees in the given age and marital status group. Make sure that every element of the rate structure for each of the health clubs is entered as a parameter which can be modified by changing the value of a single cell.

Spreadsheet Cases

Assignment

1. Based on the descriptions and data described above, design a layout form for this application. Based on your design, develop a spreadsheet to meet Susan Santee's requirements. Be sure to test your application for accuracy and completeness. Be sure to add appropriate controls which will allow Susan to change the rate parameters associated with the three plans with minimal risk of destroying or damaging the application. Add a documentation section to your spreadsheet to make it as self-documenting as possible.

2. Write a memorandum to Susan to accompany a disk containing your spreadsheet application. This memorandum should include any instructions needed to access and run your spreadsheet. You should also discuss the key assumptions made and note any limitations you see in the data and analysis methods used.

CASE 8: Ron's Restaurant Supplies

Ron's Restaurant Supplies is a wholesaler of restaurant supplies and equipment. The business started as a supplier of coffee and coffee equipment to restaurants. Over the years Ron's has expanded its product lines to include a wide variety of nonperishable expendable restaurant supplies and restaurant equipment. Basically, if a restaurant needs it, and it doesn't need to be delivered in a refrigerated truck, Ron's supplies it.

The sales staff at Ron's Restaurant Supplies are paid on a commission basis. Sales staff receive commissions whose amount is based on three components. A percentage commission is paid on sales of supplies, a different and higher percentage commission is paid on sales of equipment, and a bonus amount is paid for each new customer found by a salesperson. The commission rates are set by the Vice President of Marketing, Ms. Nancy Evans. Ms. Evans likes to make adjustments to the commission rate structure occasionally to provide incentives in areas where growth has lagged. For instance, if equipment sales are running slow and equipment inventory is up, she may temporarily raise the commission percentage for equipment. Similarly, if she feels that the sales staff has not found enough new customers lately she may raise the bonus for new customers. When adjustments to the commission structure are made, they are effective at the beginning of the next calendar month.

Because of the complexity and changing nature of the commission system used, commissions have always been hand calculated. Ron's Restaurant Supplies uses a PC based accounting software package to handle its order processing and billing. That package is used to produce a monthly summary listing of sales of supplies, and sales of equipment for each salesperson. Each salesperson submits a list of new customers they have attracted that month and this is verified from the accounting data to determine the count of new customers. A listing for a typical month is shown below.

Ms. Evans has requested that you create a spreadsheet for her that will calculate the total commission and bonus owed to each employee. She also wants to see totals for commissions paid for sales of supplies, commissions paid for sales of equipment, and bonuses paid for attracting new customers. She asks that the

Spreadsheet Cases 53

spreadsheet be designed to allow her to easily make adjustments to any of the commission rates when needed. She indicates that she would like to be able to turn the spreadsheet over to her secretary to do the actual data entry each month. The secretary to Ms. Evans has experience in using word processing on the computer but is a novice spreadsheet user.

Application Development Notes

A set of input data for this application is shown below and is available in a spreadsheet file called **ronsdata** on your data disk. This data represents the summary sales data for the most recent month. Your spreadsheet should treat all commission and bonus rate information as parameters. That is, all uses of a given rate should reference a single cell which can be easily identified and modified by the user. Your application should contain an area displaying detailed information about commissions earned by component and salesperson, as well as, summary information for each salesperson and for the staff as whole.

Assignment

1. Based on the description above and the data provided, design a layout form for this application. Using this layout form develop a spreadsheet meeting all the requirements of this application. Make sure that your application contains appropriate control measures. Test your spreadsheet for accuracy and completeness. Add a documentation section to make your spreadsheet as self-documenting as possible.

2. Write a memorandum to Nancy Evans describing this application. Include a copy of a sample set of output based on the sample data and rates provided. A copy of a disk containing your spreadsheet application should also accompany this memorandum. Make sure that your memorandum describes a set of procedures to be used by Ms. Evans and her secretary for the entry and processing of new data each month. Make sure that your memorandum, or the spreadsheet documentation section, addresses appropriate backup and control measures.

Salesperson Name	Sales of Supplies	Sales of Equipment	New Customers
Elston, Ed	41495	42275	0
Barnes, John	50555	23006	1
Moran, Sue	52704	43011	2
Wells, Ann	45761	37530	4
Thomas, Bob	38469	39204	0
Sanders, Arnold	39071	49281	6
Lewis, Barbara	53350	48864	3
Franklin, Jim	44492	22549	4
Howell, Victor	59228	35479	4
Murray, Ben	46364	31018	5
Peterson, Pamela	37089	45134	1
Naylor, William	47067	36811	4
Owens, Louis	41575	43400	4
Garland, John	37491	29009	5
Martinez, Phil	33906	48585	3
Phelps, Brad	46146	24940	6
Darnel, Darlene	48103	49480	5
Hartlett, Gene	40793	29705	1

CASE 9: Alderson For Men

Alderson for Men is a moderate sized chain of men's clothing stores operating in the midwest. Alderson started with a single store operated in St. Louis and expanded first to additional St. Louis locations and then to other midwestern cities. At the present time there are 27 Alderson for Men stores operating in 10 cities. When Alderson's expands to a new city or opens a new store in a city already served, their philosophy is to attempt to acquire an existing men's clothing store.

Bill Alderson, CEO of Alderson for Men, has been very successful in finding good acquisitions for his company. He looks for nonchain men's clothing stores with a good customer base. He finds that there are often stores of this type which have established a good reputation in their city and are well organized and operated, but which are having trouble competing with the volume buying power of chains. When an acquisition is made, it is through a friendly takeover. Ownership of the acquired store is usually given the option of purchasing Alderson stock and an attempt is made to retain as much of the staff of the acquired store as possible.

Bill Alderson is considering expanding to a new city. Springville is a city with a population of about 120,000 which has experienced rapid population growth in recent years. Bill would like to establish a store in Springville to get a foothold in this market. Two stores in Springville have been identified as possible targets for acquisition. Financial statements for the year just completed for each of the two target stores have been obtained and are presented below.

Bill asks you to prepare a set of reports for him based on these statements. He wants to see comparisons across the target stores based on their most recent income statements and balance sheets. He also wants your report to include calculations of three key financial ratios for each target store: the current ratio, the inventory turnover rate, and a measure of return on investment. He indicates that this type of analysis is needed each time the company is considering a new acquisition.

The balance sheet and income statement categories shown below are a rather typical (though highly aggregated) set of categories for retail establishments. The financial ratios requested by Mr. Alderson my be defined as follows:

1. The current ratio for a company is simply its total current assets divided by its total current liabilities.

2. The inventory turnover rate is the number of times per year a store's inventory is turned over (sold). It is equal to the cost of goods sold from the income statement divided by the inventory amount in the asset portion of the balance sheet. (The inventory value used in computing this rate normally involves averaging the inventory level on the current balance sheet with that for the immediately prior year. Here we are assuming that the level of inventories has not changed significantly over the course of the year. Thus, we use the level of inventory at the end of the year as an estimate of average inventory throughout the year.)

3. The return on investment that Mr. Alderson is interested in is the rate of return on total owners' equity. This is equal to the net income from the income statement divided by total stockholders' equity from the balance sheet.

Since the stores involved differ significantly in size, you will use common size financial statements to facilitate comparisons between them. Common size balance sheets show the values of categories of assets, liabilities and owner's equity as a percentage of total assets. Common size income statements show the values of revenue and expense categories as a percentage of sales revenue.

Application Development Notes

The set of balance sheet and income statement data shown in the table below are also available in a spreadsheet file called **aldedata** on your data disk. You should create a reporting area of your spreadsheet that will display common-size financial statements and the requested financial ratios for the two stores in a side-by side fashion to facilitate comparisons.

Spreadsheet Cases

Assignment

1. Based on the descriptions and data provided, design a layout form for this application. Use your layout form to develop a spreadsheet which will meet the requirements for this application. Test your application for accuracy and completeness. Add a documentation section to make your spreadsheet as self-documenting as possible. Get a printed listing of the reporting section of your spreadsheet.

2. Suppose you were asked to convert this application into a spreadsheet template for use in comparing the financial statements of up to five different companies. Write a short paper describing key problems and limitations to providing such an application. Describe in general terms how you would modify your spreadsheet to allow it to be used as a general template, and describe the types of control and back-up measures that would be required for such an application.

```
FINANCIAL STATEMENTS FOR TARGET COMPANIES
```

BALANCE SHEETS COMPANY:	Knight's Menswear	Cardinal Clothing
ASSETS		
Current Assets		
Cash	$48,247	$67,532
Accounts Receivable	$67,391	$59,387
Inventory	$175,233	$146,392
Other Current Assets	$13,270	$11,341
Total Current Assets	$304,141	$284,652
Long Term Assets		
Land	$62,000	$0
Building	$178,000	$0
Equipment	$186,340	$193,240
Less: Accumulated Depreciation	($137,428)	($48,320)
Total Long Term Assets	$288,912	$144,920
TOTAL ASSETS	$593,053	$429,572

LIABILITIES

Current Liabilities		
Accounts Payable	$58,320	$73,249
Taxes payable	$23,843	$19,427
Other Current Liabilities	$2,735	$8,253
Total Current Liabilities	$84,898	$100,929
Long Term Liabilities		
Notes Payable	$55,000	$0
Other Long Term Liabilities	$0	$15,250
Total Long Term Liabilities	$55,000	$15,250
TOTAL LIABILITIES	$139,898	$116,179
Stockholders' Equity		
Paid-in Capital	$325,000	$235,000
Retained Earnings	$128,155	$78,393
Total Stockholders' Equity	$453,155	$313,393
TOTAL LIABILITIES AND STOCKHOLDERS' EQUITY	$593,053	$429,572

INCOME STATEMENTS COMPANY:	Knight's Menswear	Cardinal Clothing
SALES	$775,357	$703,228
OPERATING EXPENSES		
Cost of Goods Sold	$373,954	$362,820
Employee Wages and Benefits	$228,727	$223,627
Other Operating Expenses	$75,263	$43,635
Depreciation	$24,095	$12,215
Interest	$8,257	$2,315
Total Operating Expenses	$710,296	$644,612
PRETAX INCOME	$65,061	$58,616
Income Taxes	$22,120	$19,929
NET INCOME	$42,941	$38,687

Spreadsheet Cases

CASE 10: Numismania

Bill Giles is an avid coin collector and a trivia buff. For the amusement of himself and his friends, he has developed a trivia game in which all of the questions revolve around coins and coin collecting. Bill has played this game with several friends who are fellow coin collectors and they have all been very enthusiastic about it. In fact several of his friends have suggested that Bill should manufacture his game and sell it through advertisements in coin magazines.

Recently Bill has begun to give serious consideration to manufacturing and marketing his game. He decided to name his game Numismania and to produce and distribute it on a small scale at first to test the market. He had 100 copies of the game board and questions printed up. Then he and his family hand assembled and packaged them. He kept careful records of the materials used and amount of time required in assembly. He took his assembled games to three coin shows in nearby cities and found that Numismania generated as much interest and enthusiasm among coin collectors that he did not know as it had among his friends. He priced his game at $17.50 and soon sold out this initial production run.

Bill had included a survey form with each of the games he sold. Almost half of his purchasers returned their survey form and almost all of those who responded were very satisfied with the game. Based on this response Bill decided to do some preliminary analysis of the prospects for producing and selling his game on a larger scale. To sell his games on a large scale Bill planned to advertise in coin magazines and operate almost exclusively on a mail order basis. Bill realized that going into large scale production would require him to devote full time to this enterprise. He was sure that he could get a six month leave of absence from his job. At the end of six months he would have to either resign or return to work. Bill decided to develop revenue and cost estimates for six months of operation. If he decided to proceed with this venture he would initially commit for only six months. He would assess sales and profitability during that period before making a decision to quit his job.

Bill proceeded to get estimates of the costs associated with this venture. He consulted several local printers to get an estimate of the best available price for the printing of the game boards and question cards. He investigated the costs of other raw materials, packaging materials and supplies, and shipping. He also developed estimates of labor costs for assembling, packaging, and shipping games and for processing orders. He examined plant facilities available for rent that could be used as a manufacturing and warehouse facility for his operations. Finally, he developed estimates of the costs of renting the equipment that would be needed to support the assembly, marketing, and shipment of his game. Bill divided his cost estimates into fixed costs and variable costs. Bill's estimates of the cost components are shown in the table below.

Fixed costs are costs which do not vary with the number of units (games) produced and sold. Bill developed estimates of the total amount of those costs. Among the costs he considered fixed were the cost of renting a plant facility and the cost of renting needed equipment. He also considered advertising to be a fixed cost. He would need to place ads in the three most prevalent magazines for coin collectors. He planned to place quarter page ads and, to get favorable rates, he would need to commit to run those ads for the full six months, the costs of this would be $13,200 as shown below. He also considered his salary as manager of the operation to be a fixed cost. He would have to give up the salary and benefits from his regular job for six months to manage this venture. He estimated that he would be giving up $28,000 in salary and benefits, so he listed that amount as his manager's salary.

Variable costs are those costs which vary in proportion to the level of output. Bill estimated these costs on a per game produced basis. Bill felt that he could use unskilled labor for virtually all of his operations and that it would be relatively easy to adjust the amount of labor employed in proportion to changes in the required amount of production. The other variable cost elements shown are, for the most part expendable materials whose level of usage, and cost, should be proportional to the number of units produced.

Spreadsheet Cases

Numismania Game Cost Estimates

Variable Costs (Per Game Produced):

Assembly Labor	$1.15
Printing Costs	$2.45
Raw Materials	$1.22
Packing and Shipping Labor	$0.80
Packing Materials	$0.57
Shipping Costs	$1.20
Order Processing / Secretarial Labor	$1.05
Supplies / Miscellaneous	$0.75

Fixed Costs (Total for Six Month Period):

Manager's Salary	$28,000.00
Advertising	$13,200.00
Plant Rental	$15,000.00
Equipment Lease	$7,200.00

Bill is uncertain about how to price his game. It seemed to sell quite well at the $17.50 price he used when testing sales at the coin shows. He does not think he should price his game higher then $25. He wants to compare the number of units he would have to sell to break even at the original $17.50 price with the number of units required to break even at higher prices, such as $20, $22.50 and $25.

Bill asks you to develop a spreadsheet for him that will help him assess the profit potential of his idea. He would like to see reports and/or graphs showing the breakeven point for his business at each of the alternative prices he has proposed. He would also like to see a report or graph showing the level of profit or loss earned at various levels of units sold for each alternative price. He believes that 20,000 units in a six month period is the maximum number of units he could produce with the plant and equipment he will be using. So he wants to see the projected profit or loss for various level of units sold up to 20,000.

Bill sees this as a one shot application. There may be a need to adjust some of the cost figures, but if that occurs Bill will come to you to have you recalculate the spreadsheet. He knows nothing about spreadsheets and wants to receive output only in the form of printed reports or graphs.

This project requires that you be able to compute the level of profit or loss and the breakeven point for an enterprise. The level of profit is simply equal to total revenue minus total cost. Total revenue is equal to sales price times units sold and total cost is equal to total fixed cost plus per unit variable costs times the number of units sold. That is profit equals:

Sales Price X Units Sold - (Fixed Cost + Per Unit Variable Cost X Units Sold)

To calculate the breakeven point one must first determine the contribution margin for each unit sold. The contribution margin is simply the price per unit minus the sum of variable costs per unit. Total fixed costs are computed by summing up all of the fixed cost elements. Then the breakeven point is determined by dividing total fixed costs by the contribution margin. That is, the breakeven quantity equals:

$$\frac{\text{Total Fixed Costs}}{\text{Sales Price - Per Unit Variable Cost}}$$

Application Development Notes

Because of the small amount of input data used for this application, no data file is provided. You should create a section or worksheet page for the cost values shown in the table above and including calculations of total fixed and variable costs. Your spreadsheet should also include a separate section or worksheet page with one row or column for each of the sales price alternatives. For each alternative the contribution margin and the breakeven point should be computed and shown. You should also show gross profit or loss estimates for each sales price at a variety of levels of units sold up to 20,000. You should also provide an appropriate set of graphs highlighting key features of your results.

Spreadsheet Cases

Assignment

1. Based on the description and data provided, design a layout form for this application including any graphs you will be using. Based on your layout form develop a spreadsheet to meet all of the requirements of this application. Test your application for accuracy and completeness.

2. Write a memorandum to Bill Giles. Incorporate your key reports and graphical results in this memorandum and highlight the most important features of your results.

Handwritten notes:

Contribution Margin = $/unit − VC/unit

P = TR − TC
TR = SP × units sold
TC = TFC + VC × units sold
∴ P = SP × units sold − (FC + per Unit VC × units sold)

BE =

CHAPTER 3: DEVELOPING DATABASE APPLICATIONS

In this chapter we will describe design and development tools and methods which are appropriate for simple database applications. Much of the development process described in Chapter 1 applies, not just to spreadsheet applications, but to the development of all types of applications. However, we will see that there are some unique features to database applications which require some variations in the development process used. Before discussing the development process for database applications in detail, we will first discuss the relative strengths and weaknesses of spreadsheet and database software packages. This should give you a feel for making decisions about which type of software to use for a particular application.

CHARACTERISTICS OF SPREADSHEET AND DATABASE PACKAGES

When a choice of software packages is available, it is important that the developer select the package, or combination of packages, that is best suited for the application that is to be developed. Thus, it is appropriate at this point to briefly discuss the capabilities and limitations of spreadsheets and database management packages.

Spreadsheet and database management packages are each capable of producing completed applications. Often you will need to choose the package which is most appropriate for a particular application. In other cases it may make sense to use a database package for one portion of an application and a spreadsheet for another portion.

Although both spreadsheets and database packages have capabilities in all of the key areas required for an application (output, input, processing, storage, and control), each has distinct strengths and weaknesses. A list of key strengths of spreadsheet and database packages is shown in Figure 3-1.

Spreadsheets have an intuitive user interface which is often easier for end users to grasp and work with than the interface offered by database packages. Spreadsheets

Figure 3-1

A Comparison of Key Capabilities of
Spreadsheet and Database Packages

KEY SPREADSHEET FEATURES

1. Provides an intuitive and user friendly interface that is easy for users to work with in building applications.

2. Allows relatively complex mathematical and statistical computations to be performed including comparisons of individual and summary values.

3. Allows extensive user interaction with applications and user control of parameters for "what if" analysis.

4. Allows very flexible formatting and layout of data for reporting.

5. Allows presentation of results in graphical form.

6. Allows the rapid entry and use of small amounts of data which do not need to be maintained for repeated long term use.

KEY DATABASE FEATURES

1. Allows controlled entry and maintenance of data that is needed for sets of data that will be accumulated and used over time.

2. Allows data to be made available in a variety of sorted orders that might be required for different applications.

3. Allows summarized or selected data to be quickly and easily provided when needed for reporting purposes.

4. Allows logically related data from multiple files to be linked together.

5. Allows the same data to be used, in different forms and sorted in different ways, in a variety of different output documents.

Developing Database Applications 67

also feature strong and flexible processing capabilities that allow one to quickly perform varied mathematical and statistical computations. They allow great flexibility in the layout and formatting of results for reporting and provide graphical output capabilities. Spreadsheets can provide users with strong what-if capabilities by allowing them to interact with and control their applications. Users can quickly make changes to parameters and immediately see the effects of those changes.

Limitations of spreadsheets mainly revolve around their handling of data. Spreadsheets are not particularly effective in handling large amounts of data that may need to be collected over a period of time, and used later. It is also difficult to use a spreadsheet in situations where a common set of data or selected portions of a common set of data need to be used to produce many different reports.

These data handling capabilities are the main strength of database management software. Database packages are designed to accommodate the entry and maintenance of data in table structures created by application components that are separate from the report and query components of an application that are developed to produce outputs. Depending on the database software package used, these structures may be stored as seperate files or they may be separate named objects within an overall database file. We will use the term object to refer to these components. The data entry environment for database packages makes its easy to enter data either in a batch mode or one record at a time as it becomes available. The data entry environment provided also has the ability to automatically detect many types of errors and forms can be created to further facilitate and enhance data entry. Since separate objects are used to perform the processing needed to produce reports or other output, it is easy for one set of data to be used for several applications producing a variety of different outputs.

Database packages also allow the linking together of logically related data that may have been stored in separate files. Many database applications require the use of multiple linked tables of data. The cases presented in this casebook are designed so that each case can be developed using only single data table. However, specifications for developing multi-table versions of several of the cases are also provided. Your instructor may require you to complete one or more of the cases using multiple linked tables. In describing the development process for database applications, we will initially assume that a single table is used. A later section of this chapter will describe the changes required when multiple related tables are used.

Database packages also have significant processing capabilities. Processing that requires summarization of data, sorting of data, or selection of data can be accomplished quite readily by a database package, and often these applications are better suited to database packages than to spreadsheets. The querying capabilities built into database software make it particularly effective in dealing with unanticipated, ad-hoc, requests for selected information that has been gathered to satisfy the needs of other applications.

At the same time several important processing capabilities available in spreadsheets are not supported by most common database packages. Database packages typically do not have the capability to handle many of the complex mathematical and statistical computations found in spreadsheet software. Database software cannot handle situations in which summary information is used to create a computed field for each individual record, such as a comparison of each individual's score to the average score for a group. Database packages typically cannot handle situations in which "if" logic is used to calculate the values for a field in a report. Finally, many database packages, including DBASE, do not support the production of graphical output.

Based upon these characteristics, we can make some generalizations about the types of applications that can best be developed using database software. Applications which have strong requirements for the storage and maintenance of a set of data to support varied uses should be developed using database software. Applications which require complex computations performed on relatively small volumes of data are better suited to spreadsheet development.

Of course, some applications require capabilities that are best provided by using spreadsheet and database software together. For example, data may be stored and maintained in database files. Then selected or summarized data may be retrieved from the database in a form readable by a spreadsheet package. A spreadsheet may then be used to provide flexible computational capabilities, the manipulation of

Developing Database Applications

parameters, and the ability to produce graphical output. Application software product "suites" often allow data from a database to be linked into a spreadsheet. The values of certain spreadsheet cells are defined as formulas that reference specified data from a related database table. When this type of linkage is used, changes to data in the database table will automatically appear in the related spreadsheet file the next time it is accessed.

In the remainder of this chapter we will describe some design and development tools and methods that are appropriate for database oriented applications. We will also briefly discuss the design and development of applications requiring the integrated use of database and spreadsheet packages. To facilitate this discussion, a case suitable for development as a database application is presented below. We will then describe the development process in the context of that case.

THE TEES ARE WE CASE

Tees Are We is a supplier of T-Shirts to athletic teams and other groups. Tees Are We produces its shirts to order and guarantees delivery within 3 working days. All orders placed must be for a total of at least 15 shirts. Customers may select from a number of predefined designs or may request a custom design. Four sizes (small, medium, large, and extra large) are available. Only one design is allowed for each order, but a variety of shirt sizes may be requested on a single order. For example, a customer could place an order for 5 medium, 12 large, and 3 extra large shirts of a particular pattern.

Tees Are We has always used a manual order system. The necessary information for processing an order is recorded on an order form. This information includes the customer's name and phone number, the order date, the number of units of each size ordered, and the design selected. Customers can select predefined designs from a design book. The design number of the selected design is then recorded on the customer's order form. If a custom design is desired a drawing of the design is made and approved by the customer and this drawing is attached to his or her order.

A copy of each new order is placed at the bottom of a stack of pending orders. Orders are filled one at a time from the top of the stack of pending orders. The shirt printing machine is set up to imprint the selected design for each order as it is processed in turn. This method ensures that orders are filled in the order that they were placed, but it does not necessarily lead to efficiency in production.

In particular, the store manager has noticed that there are often multiple pending orders requesting the same design. Set up time could be reduced if all of these orders could be filled with a single production run. The manager also has had difficulty in controlling his inventory of shirts of different sizes. Deliveries are sometimes delayed due to shortages of some shirt sizes, while other shirt sizes are substantially overstocked. Information about the number of units of each shirt size needed to satisfy each day's pending orders would help him do a better job of managing his shirt inventory. The manager of Tees Are We would like us to develop a computer application to address these problems.

ANALYSIS

Analysis of a potential end user application seeks to identify the requirements the application must meet with respect to each of the fundamental components of an information system. Those components were described in Chapter 1. We seek to identify the output, input, processing, storage, control, and user interface requirements of the application.

For the applications we have designed thus far, it has not been necessary to record the results of the analysis stage in written form. However, as the size and complexity of applications increase it becomes increasingly important to have written notes of the key requirements of an application. The form in which these requirements are recorded will depend upon the complexity of the application and the skills and needs of its developer and users. Figure 3-2 shows an example of an Application Requirements Report that might be used for the Tees Are We case. This report simply records, in summary narrative form, the requirements of the application with respect to each of the major information system components. It serves as a guide for use during design and implementation to ensure that all of the requirements are met. This type of information should be sufficient to document the requirement of most end-user

Developing Database Applications

developed applications.

For the Tees Are We case, two formal outputs need to be produced: a report listing all pending orders, sorted by design type, for use in managing production runs, and a report listing the total number of shirts of each size ordered on each day. The third item listed under output in Figure 3-2 relates to ad-hoc reporting needs and is described further below.

Input data for the application are supplied by the customer as each order is placed and these data need to be stored in an organized fashion for later retrieval. We will have to ensure that enough information is gathered from the customer to allow the required output to be produced, and that this information is stored effectively. The transformation processes required are relatively simple. Data must be sorted in the appropriate order for each output report and individual data values must be added to produce summary totals.

Control and user interface requirements are an important consideration for this application. The data used in this application are not of a personal or sensitive nature and, thus, access controls are not required. However, this application stores and maintains important organizational data. Thus, it will be necessary to establish procedures for making back-up copies of the application's files. Also portions of this application will be used by individuals with limited computer experience. Ideally, sales staff should be able to enter a new order record as each order is placed. They will need a simple user interface and step by step instructions describing how they are to use the application. Also, we likely will want them only to perform data entry activities. Other activities, such as correcting errors in records that have been created and deleting records for orders that have been filled (or migrating them to another file), should be the responsibility of one individual who has a good working knowledge of the software used to implement the application.

Analysis of Ad-hoc Output Needs. The ability to produce ad-hoc output whose specific nature cannot be determined in advance is an important feature of database applications. For example, the manager of Tees Are We might discover that a particular design has been lost or damaged, or that he is out of one size of shirt and

Figure 3-2

Application Requirements Report
for the Tees Are We Case

Output Requirements

A report of pending orders sorted and subtotaled by Design Type is to be produced.

A summary report showing the number of shirts of each size ordered on each order date is to be produced.

Support should be provided for ad-hoc retrievals of names and phone numbers of selected customers whose orders have various characteristics.

Input Requirements

All input data are to be obtained from customers during the order taking process.

Processing Requirements

Required processing includes sorting on design type and order date respectively and calculating some totals and subtotals.

Storage Requirements

Input data are to be collected as each order is placed, and stored for periodic reporting. Data for each order will be retained until that order is filled.

Control / User Interface Requirements

Sales staff are to input data for new orders only.

Corrections, Report generation, and deletion or migration of filled orders are to be performed only by the manager or the assistant manager in the manager's absence.

A back-up copy of the pending orders data file is to be made at noon and just prior to closing each day.

Developing Database Applications

will not be able to get a shipment for several days. In either event, he would like to be able to quickly retrieve a listing of pending orders affected by the problem, so that he can contact the affected customers.

Database applications should be designed to provide maximum support for this kind of ad-hoc reporting. The actual production of ad-hoc reports is accomplished using the data retrieval capabilities of database packages to retrieve selected data from a stored database as the need arises. Although we cannot predetermine which specific design type or shirt size the manager will want to inquire about, we can anticipate the *type* of information that will be needed and insure that the application that is developed stores and maintains the kinds of data that users are likely to need to retrieve on an ad-hoc basis. For example, in the Tees Are We case, neither of the prespecified output reports necessarily requires that the customer's phone number be input and stored in the database. However, in our analysis of the application, we would anticipate the types of ad-hoc output needs that are likely to arise and provide the kinds of data required to fulfil those needs. Thus, we would be sure to include the customer's phone number in the input data to be collected and stored. The final entry under *output* in Figure 3-2 describes this requirement.

Software Selection. Normally the decision about the type of software package to be used to develop an application is made immediately after the analysis of the application's requirements has been completed. This application is clearly one that can best be developed using database software. It uses data that need to be placed in computerized form as each order is received and that data must be maintained for periodic reporting. It involves multiple output reports, which are derived from the same set of data. In addition, users are likely to need to retrieve selected portions of the stored data for ad-hoc reporting. Finally, it has only very simple processing requirements which can easily be handled by database software.

DESIGN

The design of an application provides a visual representation of the elements needed to meet an application's requirements. The design should provide a pattern for the actual implementation of the application. For spreadsheet applications, all application components could be implemented by a single spreadsheet file. Thus, we were able to represent the entire design of the application using one design tool, the layout form.

Database applications use a diverse set of component objects. First there is a process for creating a table. Creating a table actually creates and stores a definition of how a table is organized - things like what data fields are to be stored and their data type and length. This defines the structure that is used to collect *input* records and to *store* data. Once the table structure is defined, data must still be entered into the table using standard data entry features of the database software, or through the use of forms. Often it is necessary to *process* the data stored in a table and convert it into the format desired for *output* reporting. Reports are created to perform these functions. Several different reports may be developed from a single table. Each report is created as a separate object. The layout forms we described in Chapter 1 are a good tool for describing the processing and output requirements that will be implemented by report files. However, the layout form is not a good tool for describing the table structure specifications needed to support database input and storage requirements. Here the key need is to define the structure of the data to be collected and stored. A design tool which we will call the Data Dictionary Form can be used to record this type of information.

DATA DICTIONARY FORMS

As we have already noted, database management software is normally used when there is a need to store and maintain data in an organized fashion to support the production of multiple types of output. Databases are designed to work with groups of data that can be thought of as fitting into a table structure. This table structure also corresponds to a standard file structure. That is, there are a number of instances of something (a person or thing) that we are gathering data about, and we must be gathering the same set of characteristics for each instance. In the Tees Are We case, we are gathering information about orders that are placed and we are interested in the same characteristics (Order Number, Order Date, Customer Name, Customer's Phone Number, Design Type, and the number of Units Ordered of each size of shirt) for each order. A sample of data for the Tees Are We case is shown in Figure 3-3. The

Developing Database Applications

Figure 3-3

Table of Sample Data
for the Tees Are We Case

Order Number	Order Date	Customer's Name	Customer's Phone Number	Design Type	Units Ordered Sm.	Med.	Lge.	Extra Lge.
1001	09/28/96	Barnes, Janet	774-3826	M32861	2	10	8	4
1002	09/28/96	Jones, Ed	525-1834	CUSTOM	0	17	22	14
1003	09/28/96	Adams, Al	779-8921	R38671	26	14	0	2
1004	09/28/96	Davis, Owen	523-3826	M32861	0	73	44	32
1005	09/28/96	Landes, Larry	775-2913	CUSTOM	10	7	3	0
1006	09/29/96	Morris, Sue	778-8371	P22371	0	8	16	4
1007	09/29/96	Bates, Nancy	773-6018	CUSTOM	28	0	0	0
1008	09/29/96	Thomas, Rob	526-9205	P22371	0	18	14	7
1009	09/29/96	Date, Charles	777-9014	R38671	16	11	3	0
1010	09/30/96	Evans, Jim	523-0145	M32861	4	31	11	6
1011	09/30/96	Lewis, John	778-2891	CUSTOM	0	0	7	34

characteristics that are recorded for each instance correspond to the field names in a file structure or the column names in the table display of Figure 3-3. Each instance corresponds to a record in a file structure or a row in our table display.

Database software requires that we define the column structure of a table before we begin to collect and store data in it. Information about the structure of a table is commonly known as *data dictionary* information. The amount of information in a data dictionary can vary.

Figure 3-4 shows a simple data dictionary form for a table that might have been used to store the data in the Tees Are We case. At the top of the form the name of the table (**ORDER** in this case) is recorded. Below the table name, there is an indication of control measures to be used when entering and maintaining the data of this table. Here we note that anyone on the sales staff is allowed to create a new order, but only the manager is to be allowed to modify or delete orders that have been created. Following the description of controls a set of information describing each column is presented. The information to be specified for each column includes:

Figure 3-4

Data Dictionary Form
for the Tees Are We Case

TABLE NAME: ORDER

REQUIRED CONTROLS FOR ACCESS AND USE:

    Any member of the sales staff is allowed to add new order records. Only the manager or assistant manager is allowed to make corrections to order records, delete order records, or produce reports. A back-up copy of the database is to be made at noon and just prior to closing each day.

Column Name	Column Description	Data Type and Length	Indexed?
Ord#	Assigned order number from printed order pad, must be unique	Character 5	yes unique
Ord_Date	Date when order was placed in mm/dd/yy format	Date	yes nonunique
Cust_Name	Name of the customer placing this order	Character 20	no
Cust_Phone#	Phone number of customer	Character 8 e.g. 999-9999	no
Design_Type	Number of design selected from the design book or "Custom" if a custom design has been selected	Character 6	yes nonunique
Sm-Units	Number of size small shirts ordered	Numeric 4.0	no
Med_Units	Number of size medium shirts ordered	Numeric 4.0	no
Lg_Units	Number of size large shirts ordered	Numeric 4.0	no
XLg_Units	Number of size extra-large shirts ordered	Numeric 4.0	no

Developing Database Applications

1. A name for the column in a format that is acceptable for implementation using database software,

2. A definition or description of the data item,

3. An indication of the type and dimensions of the data to be stored in the column, and

4. an indication of whether or not the table should be indexed on this column of data.

The column names used are short and contain no blank spaces since field names used by most database software cannot contain spaces and are restricted in length. These abbreviated names can be confusing in some instances, so it is important that we have column descriptions which can describe the data in greater detail.

The data type helps determine how data will be stored and used by the database software. The most commonly used data types are: character, numeric, and date. The *character* data type is used for alphabetic data and can be used for variables containing numeric digits, such as social security numbers, when they will never be used mathematically. The *numeric* data type is used for numeric data of all types that will be used in mathematical computations. The *date* data type is a special data type used just for dates.

The length specified for a column should be large enough to accommodate the largest or lengthiest entry we ever expect to use for that column. For numeric columns we indicate both the length and the number of places required after the decimal point. The value **4.0,** shown as the length for the S_UNITS column, indicates that the column is four digits long with no digits after the decimal point. Columns with a date data type normally do not require a length specification because the database software provides a fixed length for them.

The last item recorded for each column is an indication of whether or not an index is needed for the column and, if there is an index, whether or not it should be unique. An index allows us to quickly retrieve data from the table sorted in order based on the value of the column. However, maintaining indexes consumes storage space and processing time. Thus, an index should be maintained on a column only if it is used as an identifier for rows (records) in the table, or if we will frequently need to sort the data in order based on that column. The column (or columns) used for identification is called the *primary key* and a unique index should always be created for the primary key column. In the Tees Are We case, a unique Ord# is assigned to each order and this ORD# is used to identify a particular order record. In the Tees Are We case, We also need to produce one report that is sorted on DESIGN_TYPE and another that is sorted on ORD_DATE. Thus, we will also want to create indexes on each of these columns. However, these indexes are not unique. That is, different orders are allowed to have the same DESIGN_TYPE or ORD_DATE. These indexes are used to identify sets of orders with a characteristic in common. At the same time, the unique index on ORD# assures that no two orders will be assigned the same ORD#.

LAYOUT FORMS

Layout forms for database applications provide information very similar to that described for spreadsheet applications in Chapter 1. A separate layout form will be used for each independent output to be produced by the application. Sample layout forms for the two reports in the Tees Are We case are shown in Figures 3-5 and 3-6. The data source to be used with a report is indicated above the heading in the layout form. This area describes any sort or selection operations which should be performed on the table before the report is produced. Typically, the report will be based on a query that performs the selection operations on the table which are described under DATA SOURCE in Figures 3-5 and 3-6. For the examples shown, data need to be sorted to support grouping of the data. Boxed areas of the layout forms will contain data values retrieved or computed from the table or query. The format of these data values and descriptions of how they are to be obtained appear in the boxes (or, when necessary in brackets following the boxed area). The nonboxed information on the layout forms represents literal labels that should appear on the reports. The descriptions presented describe sorting or grouping activities and computation of subtotals and totals, since these are the processing activities for these reports.

Developing Database Applications

CODING

When analysis and design have been completed it is time to create your application in computerized form. This is accomplished by typing the sets of instructions and entering the data required to implement the application using an appropriate database management software package.

Details of the instructions required to implement applications will not be described here. For most database applications you will need to follow a set of steps in sequence to code or implement your design. First, create the structure of your

---

Figure 3-5

Layout Form for the Tees Are We Case Production Scheduling Report

DATA SOURCE: ORDER Table sorted by design type.

```
                    Pending Orders by Design Type

    Order  Order     Customer         Units      Units      Units      Units
    Number Date      Name             Size       Size       Size       Size
                                      Small      Medium     Large      Ex. Large

                                    ┌─ 1st value
    Design Type   │CUSTOM│         ─┤  of grouping
                                    └─ variable

   ┌─────────────────────────────────────────────────────────────────────────┐
   │ 1002  09/28/96  Jones, Ed        0          17         22         14    │
   │                                                                         │
   │ (data from the corresponding column of ORDER table                      │
   │   - for the first Design Type)                                          │
   └─────────────────────────────────────────────────────────────────────────┘

    Subtotal                        ┌─────────────────────────────┐
                                    │ (Subtotal of column above)  │
                                    └─────────────────────────────┘
          .           .        .        .         .          .
          .           .        .        .         .          .
          .           .        .        .         .          .

    Total                           ┌─────────────────────────────┐
                                    │ (Total of column Above)     │
                                    └─────────────────────────────┘
```

Figure 3-6

**Layout Form for the Tees Are We Case
Report of Daily Orders by Shirt Size**

DATA SOURCE: ORDER Table sorted and grouped by Order Date.

Units of Shirts Required for Pending Orders
by Order date and Shirt Size

Order Date	Units Size Small	Units Size Medium	Units Size Large	Units Size Ex. Large	
09/28/96	28	63	122	63	Data values from query grouped by order date
09/29/96	37	55	108	72	
.	.	.	.	.	
.	.	.	.	.	
.	.	.	.	.	
TOTAL	9999	9999	9999	9999	Total of column above

---

table following the design provided by your data dictionary form. Be sure to create any indexes needed for any sorted reports that will be required. Next, perform data entry operations to gather the data to be stored in your table. Once your table is populated with at least a sample of data you can create the query and report objects required for your application.

You may want to create a special "form" to use when adding or modifying records in your table. Forms are another type of component or object that can be created as a part of database applications. Forms help to improve the speed, accuracy, and user friendliness of the data entry process. Where there is a limited number of possible values for a column in a table, a list of possible values can be displayed and the user selects from the list. This is easier for the user and reduces data entry errors. Such a list might be used for the Design_Type column of the Tees Are We case.

A layout form similar to that shown for reports is an appropriate design tool for use in designing sophisticated data entry forms. However, for the cases presented here, we will assume that no layout form designs are needed for data entry forms.

Developing Database Applications 81

Data are to be entered using standard editing structures of the database package or through forms whose design can be derived from the data dictionary information for the table.

To test your familiarity with fundamental database operations, you should build the table, queries, and reports required to implement the Tees Are We case. If you are using DBASE or ACCESS, you can check your work against the sample files provided on the data disk. DBASE files are provided in a subdirectory called DBTRW and the ACCESS version is in a file called TRW.MDB.

TESTING METHODS

The database table structures created by an application and any forms, queries, and reports produced need to be tested for accuracy. Database table structures and input forms are tested by inputing sample data. The data type and length defined for each field should be appropriate for the storage of all values that the field can take on. A set of sample data including extreme values for various fields should be used for testing.

Queries and reports need to be checked for the accuracy of the results they produce in the same way that spreadsheet files are tested. The computations performed by the query or report are checked by performing manual calculations for the set of test data. It is particularly important to check subtotals within reports to make sure that the data used by the report has been sorted and grouped correctly.

In addition to testing for accuracy, applications should also be tested for clarity and completeness. Do the set of outputs produced meet all of the requirements of the application? Are the heading and labels easy to understand? Do they fully describe the data that are presented? These questions should be addressed in testing the application. As inaccuracies or limitations are discovered they are corrected and the application is retested until the user or set of users of the application are satisfied with its performance.

DOCUMENTATION

As we discussed in Chapter 1, creating documentation is an important part of the development of any application. Database applications are almost always maintained over a period of time and often are operated by multiple users. These features make documentation particularly crucial for database applications. Database table structures are automatically self-documenting to some extent, because a first time user can look up data dictionary information on a table to identify the fields involved and the type of data stored. However, with database packages it is not feasible to add a comment section of the type we placed in our spreadsheet files. Database applications normally require some external written documentation describing the procedures to be followed by their users. This documentation should also provide instructions for the control of the database and procedures for making periodic backup copies of your database file.

Figure 3-7 shows a set of procedures that might be used for the Tees Are We case. The procedures presented assume that the application was developed using ACCESS. Notice that a very explicit and detailed set of instructions is provided for the order clerks who will be using the system. The instructions describing how the manager and assistant manager are to use the application are much less detailed because we are assuming that these individuals will have a good understanding of fundamental aspects of the ACCESS software package.

INTEGRATED APPLICATIONS

As we noted earlier, many applications can best be handled by a combination of database and spreadsheet software. Most frequently we may have an application using data that need to be collected and stored over a period of time, but which requires analysis using complex computations or requires output displayed in graphical form. Such an application would best be handled by creating a database file to collect and store the needed data. Then, when analysis is needed, the database file could be exported to or linked to a spreadsheet. This data could then be manipulated using all of the features of spreadsheet software.

Developing Database Applications 83

Figure 3-7

Documentation of User Procedures for the Tees Are We Case

ORDER CLERKS

1. Accessing the Table. This process is to be used every morning to initially access the order table, and each time you need to access the order table after doing some other computer operation.
    A. Select the **ACCESS** icon from the opening window.
    B. Pick the **Open Database** icon
    C. Select the database name **TRW.MDB** from the list of choices
    D. Click on the **Tables** icon and the **Order** table.
    E. Select **Open** to display this table in a datasheet view that permits the entry of new order records.

2. Entry of order data.
    A. You should see a blank data form for the Order table on your screen. Key in the appropriate data for each order as you process it and use the tab key to move to the next column.
    B. Before pressing the enter key after filling the last row of the form, double check all of your data and make any corrections that are needed.
    C. Press enter to save the completed record and produce a blank screen for the next order.
    D. If you mistakenly save an order record with erroneous data, have the manager or assistant manager make the needed correction.

3. Making backup copies of the database. A backup copy of the Order table is to be made at noon and just after the last order is processed each day.
    A. Open the **File Manager** window.
    B. **COPY** the **TRW.MDB** file to a file called **A:TRWBAK.MDB** on the floppy diskette labelled database backup.
    D. Use part 1 instructions to get back into the order file if more orders are to be processed.

ASSISTANT MANAGER AND MANAGER

1. You can retrieve and print two reports one called TRWDES which summarizes orders by design type and another called TRWDATE which summarizes pending orders for each shirt size on a daily basis.

2. Get a list of filled orders from production at the close of each day and migrate those orders out of the orders database file.

3. Periodically check the creation date of the backup file **A:TRWBAK.MDB** to ensure that backup procedures are being followed.

In designing the layout forms for the spreadsheet application, the input area would be described as being derived from the associated database file.

In implementing this type of integrated application, the database file would be created, populated, and tested first. Then data would be exported to or linked to a spreadsheet to create a spreadsheet file containing a copy of the data extracted from the database. Finally, the spreadsheet formulas needed to produce the spreadsheet outputs would be created and tested to complete the application.

BUILDING MULTI-TABLE DATABASE APPLICATIONS

One of the most powerful features of database software packages is their ability to support applications using multiple related tables. When we described the Tees Are We case, we indicated that customers select designs from a design book. Only a DESIGN_TYPE code was recorded in our ORDER table. However, we can easily imagine that each design has a number of characteristics which could be recorded in a database table. Let us suppose, for instance, that there is a text description for each design and that there is a price for each design - some designs are more elaborate than others and thus their price is higher.

We could simply add DESIGN_DESCRIPTION and PRICE columns to the ORDER table structure described in Figure 3-4. However, this approach would cause some problems. The DESIGN_DESCRIPTION and PRICE should be the same for all orders of a particular DESIGN_TYPE. For example Order Numbers 1001, 1004 and 1010 are all for the DESIGN_TYPE M32861. Suppose that the description of this design is "Wren and Stumpy" and its price is $20. We would need to type this information in for each order of the DESIGN_TYPE M32861 even though we know that the DESIGN_DESCRIPTION and PRICE should be the same for all records of this DESIGN_TYPE. This involves wasteful data entry time and increases the potential for error. A clerk might enter a DESIGN_DESCRIPTION or a PRICE incorrectly for one or more of the orders.

A more appropriate design would be one which recognizes that we have a set of information about designs that is separate from - but related to - our order information. Under this design alternative, we would create a separate DESIGN table

Developing Database Applications 85

which would have DESIGN_TYPE, DESIGN_DESCRIPTION, and PRICE as columns. The DESIGN_DESCRIPTION and PRICE for a particular design (DESIGN_TYPE) would be entered only once in this table. Figure 3-8 shows a data dictionary form for this table and Figure 3-9 shows a set of sample data.

Figure 3-8

Data Dictionary Form for the DESIGN Table

TABLE NAME: DESIGN

REQUIRED CONTROLS FOR ACCESS AND USE:

    Only the manager or assistant manager is allowed to add, change or delete records in this table. A back-up copy of this table is to be made at the close of each business week.

Column Name	Column Description	Data Type and Length	Indexed
Design_type	Number of Design from Design book or "CUSTOM" if a custom design is used	Character 6	Yes Unique
Design_Descr	Description of design	Character 30	No
Price	Retail price charged for shirts of this design from design book	Numeric 6.2	No

---

Figure 3-9

Sample Date for the DESIGN Table

Design_Type	Design_Description	Price
M32861	Wren and Stumpy	$20
CUSTOM	Customer Specified	$25
R38671	Happy Face	$15
P22371	Einstein's Relative	$20

Data from multiple tables of a database can be linked together if the tables have an attribute in common and if that common attribute is an identifying attribute in one of the tables. In our example the attribute DESIGN_TYPE is included in both the ORDER and DESIGN tables. The DESIGN_TYPE is also the primary key or identifying column in the DESIGN table. Thus, including the DESIGN_TYPE column in the ORDER table allows us to identify which row of the DESIGN table is associated with each ORDER.

DESIGN_DESCRIPTION and PRICE information can be shown for any order by creating a query which links rows of the ORDER and DESIGN tables having equal values for the DESIGN_TYPE attribute. For example, we might need to produce a report showing the order number, customer name, total number of shirts ordered, design type and description, price per unit, number of shirts ordered, and total amount billed for each order. Figure 3-10 shows a layout form for such a report, where the report also includes a total amount billed for all pending orders.

Figure 3-10

Layout Form for the Billing Summary Report

DATA SOURCE: Query Linking the ORDER and Design Tables

Summary of Billings for Pending Orders

```
Order      Customer    Design    Design                              Qty.   Amount
Number     Name        Type      Description              Price      Ord.   Billed

  1001    Jones, Ed   M32861    Wren and Stumpy           $20         24     $480
    (data from the corresponding column of ORDER or Design)
       (Defined as S_QTY + M_QTY + L_QTY + XL_QTY in query)
       (Defined as (S_QTY + M_QTY + L_QTY + XL_QTY) * Price in query)

   TOTAL
                                      (Total of Amount Billed Column)
```

Developing Database Applications

In a typical database package, most of the computational work of this report can be accomplished in the query that is used as its input. The required query would link or join the ORDER and DESIGN tables based on the condition that the value of DESIGN_TYPE is equal across the two tables. Displayed columns would include the ORD#, ORD_DATE, and CUST_NAME columns from the ORDER table and the DESIGN_TYPE, DESIGN_DESCRIPTION, and PRICE columns of the DESIGN table. The query would also include a computed field summing the number of shirts of all sizes ordered (=SM_UNITS + MED_UNITS + LG_UNITS + XLG_UNITS) and another computed field to calculate the total amount billed for the order. We are assuming no taxes or other added charges and no volume discounts. Thus, this field will equal (SM_UNITS + MED_UNITS + LG_UNITS + XLG_UNITS)*PRICE. Figure 3-11 shows what the results of this query would look like for the sets of sample data shown in Figures 3-2 and 3-9.

Sample files showing the multi-table implementation of the Tees Are We case are available in DBASE form in a subdirectory called DBTRWM and in ACCESS form in a file called TRWM.MDB on your data disk. Build this application yourself and compare your results to those on the data disk.

Figure 3-11

Sample Query Results Linking ORDER and DESIGN Tables

Order Number	Customer's Name	Design Type	Design Description	Price	Qty. Ord.	Amount Billed
1001	Barnes, Janet	M32861	Wren and Stumpy	$20	24	$ 480
1002	Jones, Ed	CUSTOM	Customer Specified	$25	53	$1,325
1003	Adams, Al	R38671	Happy Face	$15	42	$ 630
1004	Davis, Owen	M32861	Wren and Stumpy	$20	149	$2,980
1005	Landes, Larry	CUSTOM	Customer Specified	$25	20	$ 500
1006	Morris, Sue	P22371	Einstein's Relative	$20	28	$ 560
1007	Bates, Nancy	CUSTOM	Customer Specified	$25	28	$ 700
1008	Thomas, Rob	P22371	Einstein's Relative	$20	39	$ 780
1009	Date, Charles	R38671	Happy Face	$15	30	$ 450
1010	Evans, Jim	M32861	Wren and Stumpy	$20	52	$1,040
1011	Lewis, John	CUSTOM	Customer Specified	$25	41	$1,025

NOTE: Data tables are provided for a few of the database cases presented in Chapter 4. Where data is supplied for a case, it will be provided simply in the form of a DBASE database file (a file with a .DBF extension) or for ACCESS users, an ACCESS database (with a .mdb extension). The data provided is not indexed, nor are any additional supporting structures provided.

SUMMARY

Often you will need to choose whether to use a spreadsheet package or database package to develop an application. In other instances you may need to combine the use of a database and a spreadsheet package to produce an integrated application. Each application or application component should be developed using the type of package which best fits the work to be done. In general, database packages are best for handling sets of data that will be generated and maintained over time, used by several users, and used to produce multiple types of reports. Spreadsheet packages are best for ad-hoc, or one shot applications, for applications requiring substantial interaction, i.e. "what-if" analysis, for applications requiring complex computations, and for applications requiring graphical display of results.

The analysis stage of an end user application can be documented by an application requirements report. This report is simply a set of brief descriptions of the key output, input, processing, storage, control, and user interface requirements of an application.

For the design phase of application development layout forms similar to those described for spreadsheet applications may be used. However, design of the structure of a database file is best handled by creating a data dictionary form which describes key characteristics of the data and its structure.

Coding of database applications involves at least three phases; creation of a database file to produce the file structure, entry of sample data to populate the database file, and creation of reports file(s) to manipulate the stored data and produce desired results.

Testing of database applications has several elements. We must ensure that all

Developing Database Applications 89

reasonable data values are accepted by the system and stored properly, ensure that all computations performed are correct, and ensure that data are indexed properly to support reports requiring sorted data, and ensure that all requirements of the system are met.

Database applications generally require more external documentation than their spreadsheet counterparts. Written documentation describing the procedures to be followed by each user of the application should be provided. The level of detail in which procedures are described should be matched to the needs of the user. Particular care should be taken to ensure that control procedures, such as procedures for making back-up copies of the database file, are well documented and fully understood.

The most common type of integrated application is one in which data are collected and stored in a database file and then copied to a spreadsheet file for analysis and display.

Many end user database applications may require the use of multiple related tables. Where this type of structure is needed, related tables are linked based on the value of a common data field which is a unique identifying field in one of the tables. Queries are created to establish these linkages and reports can be produced which are derived from these queries.

CHAPTER 4: DATABASE CASES

CASE 1: Bunyon Logging Supplies

Bunyon Logging Supplies sells chain saws and related equipment to retail customers and provides saw tune-up and repair services. Bunyon's chief competitors are department stores which sell chain saws and supplies, but do not offer repair and tune-up services. The tune-up and repair services are a key selling point. Bunyon Logging Supplies cannot match the saw prices offered by the department store, but they are able to retain a strong customer base by being a full service supplier. To drive home the advantages offered by buying a saw from them, Bunyon's offers one year of free service and repair with each new chain saw they sell.

Currently, information about the saws that have been sold is maintained manually. However, Paul Woods, manager of Bunyon Logging Supplies, would like to have a computer application that would allow him to retrieve key information about each saw Bunyon's has sold, and he has asked you to develop it for him. Paul would like to have an application that would allow him to do three key things:

1. Look up information about any saw when a customer brings it in. The information provided should include the purchase date and the date of the last servicing performed on the saw. This would allow Paul to quickly determine if a saw is under the one year service and repair agreement.

2. Retrieve a list of names and telephone numbers of customers whose year of free servicing expires within the next month and who have not yet had their saws serviced. Paul feels that calling these customers will help to build goodwill and may also get them in the habit of using his service department.

3. Retrieve a list of the names and telephone numbers of all customers whose last saw servicing was more than ten months ago. This list would be retrieved when business was slow in the service department. The customers identified would be called and offered a substantial discount if they brought their saws in

for service within a two week period. Paul feels that this would help to eliminate slack periods in the service department, and would also improve goodwill with customers.

While a substantial amount of information could be collected about each saw that is sold, Paul wants to keep the data collection as simple as possible. Data for each saw sold will be recorded by clerical staff, and many of them have no prior experience in the use of computers. Paul believes that the set of data collected for each purchase should include: the name and phone number of the purchaser, the model and identification number of the saw that was sold, the name of the salesperson who sold the saw, and the date the saw was sold. When a saw is serviced, Paul wants to record the date that the servicing was completed.

As you ask Paul Woods additional questions, you find out several important details. The customer's name can be recorded as a single field consisting of last name comma first name. The salesperson's name can be recorded in a single field as last name comma first initial. Only information about the most recent servicing is needed. When a saw is serviced for the second time, the date of the second servicing can simply replace that of the first servicing in the database. Finally, you discover that there is a five character model code for each type of saw that uniquely identifies the manufacturer and model and that the identification number for a saw is a unique code of up to ten characters.

Paul indicates that he will personally retrieve the lists of customers for servicing and for discount offers as needed. He suggests that the lists should include the model and identification number of the saw and the date of sale (or servicing) as well as the customer's name and phone number. Paul and two of his employees have enough experience with spreadsheet packages to perform ad-hoc queries. When it is necessary to retrieve the record for an individual saw or to perform some other ad-hoc retrieval, one of them will be available. To help you develop your application Paul was able to provide you with the sample set of data shown below.

Database Cases

Application Development Notes

Sample data and a set of analysis and design documents for this application are provided below. Before developing this application you should read all of this documentation carefully. The first step in implementing the application design will be to create a table whose structure corresponds to the descriptions in the data dictionary form. Once the structure of your table has been created, you will need to input the records for the set of sample data shown. When the data have been entered, you can create the two reports required for this application, using the layout forms provided as a guide. *To test your report forms using the sample data, you should assume that the current date is the first day of October, 1996 (10/01/96).*

```
                  Bunyon Logging Supplies Sample Data

Customer       Phone      Saw    Saw ID      Salesperson   Date of   Date of
Name           Number     Model  Number      Name          Sale      Last
                                                                     Service

Morris, Marie  572-4819   MC620  00748A2639  Schwartz, P.  08/17/94  06/13/95
Davis, Alvin   528-9103   ST280  4913059214  Everson, R.   10/27/94  07/04/96
Allen, Bob     762-1913   MC470  01386B7106  Everson, R.   11/02/94  04/22/95
Barnett, Ed    531-1203   ST280  3816824083  Gayle, C.     02/25/95    /  /
Clay, Art      771-0924   ST390  8140286437  Schwartz, P.  04/07/95  06/13/96
Vale, Vance    529-0187   JR340  0163V219    Everson, R.   05/17/95  04/22/96
Ward, Walter   772-1036   MC470  00748A2639  Schwartz, P.  06/04/95    /  /
Thomas, Tina   548-2106   JR690  2372B724    Gayle, C.     06/28/95  08/22/95
Dale, Dan      773-0291   ST390  1307283497  Everson, R.   08/13/95  05/06/96
Evans, John    541-0037   MC620  01023A7413  Schwartz, R.  09/23/95  08/06/96
Graves, Dan    776-9208   ST280  3701723648  Schwartz, R.  10/03/95    /  /
Frank, Fred    774-8123   JR340  0238V813    Gayle, C.     10/05/95  06/21/96
Mayfield, Max  538-2104   ST390  1427306297  Everson, R.   10/08/95    /  /
Lewis, Jan     546-8273   JR690  2864B018    Schwartz, R.  10/12/95  07/08/96
Owens, Jim     736-4813   MC470  01328A3914  Schwartz, R.  10/12/95  05/26/96
Hall, Mark     536-9110   ST280  2178309725  Everson, R.   10/16/95    /  /
Pearson, Bill  772-1936   MC620  02314A2861  Gayle, C.     10/22/95    /  /
Howell, Hal    541-6824   JR340  0316V248    Everson, R.   10/25/95  08/16/96
Jarvis, Dale   768-2464   MC470  0273645924  Schwartz, R.  10/28/95    /  /
Lyons, Will    543-7235   ST390  1672934107  Everson, R.   10/30/95    /  /
Morris, Bill   774-7423   MC620  01863A8327  Schwartz, R.  12/07/95  08/13/96
Warren, Wayne  551-9271   JR340  0566V791    Gayle, C.     01/02/96    /  /
Bailey, Al     773-8205   JR690  3648B824    Everson, R.   02/18/96    /  /
```

Assignment

1. Using the sample data and design documents provided, develop a database application which will meet all of the requirements described for this case. Be sure to test your application for completeness and accuracy.

2. Write a set of documentation to accompany this application. Your documentation should appropriately describe the procedures to be followed by all users of the system and should describe control and backup procedures to be followed.

3. To test your application's capabilities to support queries, perform the following query operations on the sample data and get printed listings of your results: A) Get a list of the names and phone numbers of customers buying MC620 model saws, B) Find the saw ID number for the saw purchased by "Morris, Marie", C) get a count of the number of saws sold by the salesperson "Schwartz, R.

Application Requirements Report

OUTPUT REQUIREMENTS

1. A report of customer information for saws sold more than 11 months and less than one year ago.

2. A report of customer information for customers whose saws were last serviced more than 10 months ago.

3. Support should be provided for ad-hoc retrievals based on customer name, saw identification number, sale or service date, salesperson name, or saw model number.

INPUT REQUIREMENTS

All input data are to be obtained by sales staff as each sale is made.

PROCESSING REQUIREMENTS

Required processing includes selecting data based on the values of selected fields.

STORAGE REQUIREMENTS

Input data are to be collected as each sale is made and are to be stored for periodic and ad-hoc reporting. Data for each sale will be retained indefinitely.

The service date is to be updated by the service staff each time servicing is performed.

CONTROL / USER INTERFACE REQUIREMENTS

Sales staff are to enter data for new sales only.

Service staff are to modify only the service date for saws they service.

All corrections to data, report generation, and querying of the database is to be performed by Paul Woods or other designated employees with experience in the use of database software.

A back-up copy of this data file is to be made by Paul Woods or a designated employee at the close of business each day.

Data Dictionary Form

TABLE NAME: SAW_SERV

REQUIRED CONTROLS FOR ACCESS AND USE:

Any member of the sales staff is allowed to add new sales records. Any member of the servicing staff is allowed to change the service date and to change the customer's phone number if required. Only Paul Woods and employees designated by him are allowed to make other changes to the data or to produce reports or queries. A back-up copy of this database is to be made at the close of business each day by Paul Woods or an employee designated by him.

Column Name	Column Description	Data Type and Length	Indexed?
Cust_Name	Name of customer stored as last name comma first name, e.g.: Smith, Adam	Character 20	No
Phone_No	Phone number of customer stored in the following format: 999-9999	Character 8	No
Saw_Model	Code identifying the manufacturer and model number of a saw, e.g.: MC620	Character 5	No
Saw_ID_No	Unique identification number of the saw sold.	Character 10	Yes unique
Slsp_Name	Name of the salesperson selling the saw stored as last name comma first initial, e.g.: Jones J.	Character 15	No
Sale_Date	Date the saw was sold in mm/dd/yy format	Date	No
Serv_Date	Date the saw was last serviced in mm/dd/yy format, value to be left null for new saws	Date	No

Database Cases

Layout Forms

Report of Customers for Initial Servicing Reminders

    Input Data to   Selected data from the SAW_SERV Table
     the Report: for sales more than 11 months and less than 1
                        year ago whose service date is null

       List of Customers to Contact for Free Saw Servicing

Customer Name	Phone Number	Saw Model	Saw Id#	Date Sold
Rivers, Richard	778-3219	ST390	6783921434	10/08/95
(data from the appropriate column of the SAW_SERV table meeting the selection criteria)				
Xxxxx, Xxxxx	XXX-XXXX	XXXXX	XXXXXXXXXX	mm/dd/yy

Report of Customers for Servicing Discount Offers

    Input Data to   Selected data from the SAW_SERV table
     the Report: for saws whose last service data is more than
                        10 months ago, but is not null

       List of Customers to Contact for Saw Servicing
                   Discount Offers

Customer Name	Phone Number	Saw Model	Saw Id#	Date Serviced
Morris, Marie	572-4819	MC620	00748A2639	06/13/95
(data from the appropriate column of the SAW_SERV table meeting the selection criteria)				
Xxxxx, Xxxxx	XXX-XXXX	XXXXX	XXXXXXXXXX	mm/dd/yy

CASE 2: The Journal-Tribune Corporation

The Journal-Tribune Corporation is the publisher of a daily newspaper in Phoenix, Arizona. In addition to publishing the daily paper, the corporation also publishes 3 specialized magazines of local interest. Auto-related air pollution and traffic congestion are serious problems in the Phoenix metropolitan area. The Journal-Tribune has taken an editorial position in support of car pooling as a method to reduce emissions and congestions. In order to demonstrate leadership in this area, June Johnson, CEO of the Journal-Tribune Corporation, wants to implement an aggressive car pooling plan within the company.

Ms. Johnson wants to encourage employees to form car pools with other Journal-Tribune employees. To assist in the forming of car pools, she wants to distribute data identifying sets of employees living in the same area of town who could potentially form a car pool.

The Journal-Tribune building is located in a congested downtown area. There is a small parking lot (50 car capacity) located under the Journal-Tribune building. Currently, senior managers are assigned parking in this lot, while all other employees must park in an uncovered lot three blocks away. As an incentive to employees to form car pools, Ms. Johnson has decided to convert the parking lot under the building to a car pool lot. Any employee who joins a car pool will be allowed to park under the building. All employees, including executives, who are not car pool members will be required to park in the uncovered lot. Each car pool member will be issued a parking permit for his/her car. The number on the parking permit will correspond to the number of the assigned parking space. The same sticker number will be assigned to each member of a car pool so that only one vehicle from each car pool will be able to park in the covered lot. A parking lot attendant will periodically monitor the lot to ensure that only cars with the appropriate permit are allowed to park in the covered lot.

Several of the reporters and sales staff have company cars assigned to them. Ms. Johnson wants to insist that staff with assigned cars join a car pool if it is reasonable for them to do so. Employees with assigned cars will be exempted from

Database Cases

the requirement to car pool only if car pooling would increase their commuting time by more than 10 minutes, or if their work and travel schedule does not allow them to participate in a car pool.

Ms. Johnson assigns you the task of implementing this car pooling scheme. She indicates that you are to prepare a memorandum for her signature to be sent to all employees describing the car pooling program. Attached to this memorandum will be a list of all Journal-Tribune employees and their addresses sorted by zip code to help identify sets of workers living in the same general area. Employees are to be asked to identify and contact fellow workers to form car pools. Workers with assigned company cars are to be notified that their continued use of those cars may depend upon joining a car pool. The parking lot under the building is to be converted to car pool use one month from the date of the memo. As employees form car pools, they are to contact you to receive permits for the lot. You are to keep a record of each employee who is issued a permit and the permit number assigned to that employee.

At the end of the one month sign up period, Ms. Johnson wants you to send her a list of all employees who have joined a car pool. She also wants to see a list of all employees who have a company car but have not joined a car pool by the implementation date. She plans to have one of her aides personally contact those employees to determine whether they qualify for exemption from the car pooling requirement.

Once the car pooling plan is in place, Ms. Johnson wants you to continue to publish lists, by zip code, of employees who are not yet members of a car pool. She wants lists to be distributed at least once a month until enough car pools are formed to fill the parking lot under the building.

To complete the task you have been assigned, you need to know the name, address, and phone number of each employee. You also need to know whether or not an employee has an assigned company car. As the car pooling plan is implemented, you will add data indicating the number of the parking sticker assigned to each employee who joins a car pool. You contact the IS department to determine what data they can provide. They indicate that they can retrieve a set of employee data for you and have it copied to a file for use with the database package on your PC. This file will include the name, address (street, city, state and zip code), office phone number, and company car status (Yes or No) for each employee. They generate a sample set of this data for 30 employees for your use in developing your application. You will receive a full, up-to-date employee list when you are ready to implement your system. A sample of this data is shown after the data dictionary form below. The full sample of 30 records is available in both a DBASE file called **car_pool.dbf** and an ACCESS file called **car_pool.mdb** on your data disk.

You plan to work with the retrieved file and to add a field to store the parking sticker assignments of employees who join car pools. For several reasons, this information will be stored in your personal database and not in the organizational database. First, the car pool plan is experimental and may change over time. Second, you will be the only user of this data, at least initially. Finally, the IS department would be unable to make the necessary changes to place this data in the organizational database within the required time frame. It is quite possible that the parking sticker information you generate may be placed in an organizational database at some future date.

Application Development Notes

Design aids for this application are presented below and a set of sample employee data records are provided for you on your data disk. Before proceeding with this application you should make a back-up copy of that file.

Your first step for this project should be to access the presupplied database table and modify its structure to include the *sticker_no* column that will store assigned car pool parking sticker numbers. Once this modification has been made, you can proceed to other considerations. Some of the reports need to be sorted by Zip Code so you should create an index on that variable. You will need to edit some of the data to add car pool sticker numbers for selected employees (as described below) in order to test some of the reports produced by this application. All reports except the first one are based on only selected records from the table. In most PC based database packages, the selection of qualifying records is accomplished by creating a query which applies the selection criteria. That query then becomes the source for the report that is created. Two of the reports require that data be grouped by zip code.

Database Cases

Remember that those reports will operate correctly only if the report is based on a query which is sorted by zip code.

Assignment

1. Based upon the descriptions above, the supplied database file, and the design documents shown below, develop an application using a database management package which meets all of the requirements described for this case. Test your application for accuracy and completeness. Write an appropriate set of documentation to accompany your application. Your documentation should be designed to support your personal use of the system or use by other individuals who are experienced in the use of database packages.

2. Make copies of all of the reports generated by this application. To produce meaningful reports for the portion of the application that utilizes car pool sticker data, you will need to assign stickers to some of the employees in the sample database. Pick at least 5 pairs of employees and assign them car pool stickers beginning with the sticker number 01. Make sure that at least two employees who have company cars are included in the set of employees getting car pool stickers.

3. There are likely to be numerous instances where querying of your database will be required. To demonstrate that your database can handle queries, retrieve the following data from your database:
    A. A count of the number of employees in car pools,
    B. The names and phone numbers of the employees who are assigned to parking sticker number 3,
    C. A list of all available data for employees in zip code 83712 who are members of a car pool.

Application Requirements Report

OUTPUT REQUIREMENTS

1. A report of employee names, addresses and phone #s grouped by zip code.

2. A report of names, addresses, and parking sticker #s of employees who have joined a car pool.

3. A report listing the names and phone #s of employees who have a company car but are not car pool members.

4. A report of names, addresses and phone #s of employees who are not yet car pool members, grouped by zip code.

INPUT REQUIREMENTS

All input data except the car pool sticker number will be supplied in a file extracted from an organizational database.

Car pool sticker number data are to be assigned when employees sign up for a car pool.

PROCESSING REQUIREMENTS

Required processing includes sorting on zip code (1, 4) and selecting subsets of the data based on whether an employee has an assigned car (3) and/or whether the employee has joined a car pool (2, 3, 4).

STORAGE REQUIREMENTS

All data except sticker numbers will be extracted at the beginning of implementation. Sticker numbers will be collected as assigned and maintained for periodic reporting. Data will be maintained indefinitely.

CONTROL / USER INTERFACE REQUIREMENTS

All data entry / corrections / report generation is to be performed by the developer or by an individual with substantial prior experience with the database package used for development.

Car pool sticker assignments are to be recorded in written form as well as being placed in the database file. A back-up copy of the car pool database file will be made at the close of each work week.

Database Cases

Data Dictionary Form

TABLE NAME: CAR_POOL

REQUIRED CONTROLS FOR ACCESS AND USE:

    This is a personal database to be used only by the developer or his/her successor.

Column Name	Column Description	Data Type and Length	Indexed?
Emp_Name	Name of Employee stored as last name comma first name, e.g. Smith, Michael	Character 15	Yes unique
Street_Add	Street Address of employee	Character 30	No
City	City of the employee's home address	Character 10	No
Zip_Code	Zip code of employee's home Address	Character 5	Yes nonunique
Wk_Phone	Employee's assigned work phone extension number	Char 4	No
Co_Car	Company car assigned to this Employee? values "Yes" or "No"	Char 3	No
Sticker_No	Assigned car pool sticker number for this employee. This field will be blank until an employee joins a car pool. Valid assigned values are 01 to 50.	Char 2	No

Sample of Supplied Data

Employee Name	Street Address	City	Zip Code	Work Ph.	Co. Car
Smith, Michael	3814 N. Pine	Tempe	83418	2822	No
Barnes, Ann	1315 N. Shea	Phoenix	83266	2319	No
Davis, Daniel	2146 N. Shea	Phoenix	83266	1623	Yes
Adams, Alvin	1978 Rural Road	Scottsdale	84082	1742	Yes
Jones, Janet	4826 W. Taft	Tempe	83418	3280	No
Tower, Bob	2214 W. Eisenhower	Phoenix	83266	1473	No
Stanton, Alice	3722 N. 35th Avenue	Phoenix	83412	3618	Yes
Flowers, Daisy	4701 N. Scottsdale Blvd.	Scottsdale	84082	1931	Yes
Downs, Dale	3817 W. Wilson	Tempe	83418	2164	No
Barrow, Carl	2807 N. 42nd Ave.	Phoenix	83412	4118	No
Lewis, Mike	2807 N. 37th Street	Phoenix	83266	3729	Yes
Mayfield, John	1728 W. Eisenhower	Phoenix	83412	1827	Yes
Owens, Linda	2214 N. Broadway	Tempe	83418	2622	Yes
Garn, Glenda	3814 N. Saguaro	Scottsdale	84082	3281	No

Application Cases in MIS

Layout Forms

Report of Employees by Zip Code Location

    Input Data to   All records of CAR_POOL table sorted by Zip Code
    the Report:

           Journal-Tribune Employees Grouped by Zip Code of Address
          for Your use in Finding Potential Car Pooling Opportunities

Employee Name	Street Address	City	Work Phone Extension #

Zip Code: [83266] ── Lowest Zip Code Value

```
Barnes, Ann    1325 N. Shea                  Phoenix        2319

  (data from the appropriate column of the CAR_POOL database file
   - with the appropriate Zip Code value)
```

Zip Code: [XXXXX] ── Next Zip Code Value

```
  (as above - data from the CAR_POOL database file - for employees
   in the next Zip Code area)
```

Report of Car Pool Membership

    Input Data to   Selected records from CAR_POOL table
    the Report: where Sticker_No is greater than zero

           Car Pool Membership List

Employee Name	Street Address	City	Car Pool Sticker #

```
Adams, Alvin    1978 Rural Road              Scottsdale       06

  (data for the appropriate column of the CAR_POOL database
   meeting the selection criterion specified above)

Xxxxxx, Xxxxx   XXXX Xxxxxx Xxxxxx           Xxxxxxxxxx       XX
```

Database Cases

Report of Non Car Pool Members Having Company Cars

    Input Data to   Selected records from CAR_POOL table
      the Report: where Co_Car = Yes and Sticker_No is not
                           greater than zero.

            List of Employees Who Have Company Vehicles
                and Are Not Yet Car Pool Members

Employee Name	Work Phone Extension #
Davis, Daniel	1623
(data for the appropriate column of the CAR_POOL database meeting the selection criteria specified)	
Xxxxx, Xxxx	XXXX

Report of Non Car Pool Members by Zip Code Location

    Input Data to   Selected records from CAR_POOL table where
      the Report: Sticker_No is not greater than zero, sorted
                          by Zip_Code

        List of Journal-Tribune Employees who are not Currently
                         Car Pool Members

> The design of the body of this report is identical to that of the Report of Employees by Zip Code Location shown above.

CASE 3: Al's Affordable Autos

Al Harper is the owner of Al's Affordable Autos, an independent used car dealership. Al purchases used vehicles at auto auctions, through agreements with several new car dealerships, and as trade-ins or direct purchases from private individuals. As the name of Al's business implies, he specializes in older lower-priced vehicles. For the most part, Al's sales are either to households looking for a second or third car or to low income households. Al operates strictly on a cash purchase basis, although he has a working agreement with a local finance company which provides financing to many of Al's customers.

Al has a staff of five salespersons. Each salesperson is paid a small salary, but the bulk of their income comes from commissions. Al pays his staff a sales commission of two percent of the sales price of the vehicle plus ten percent of the mark-up on the vehicle. Mark-up is determined as the difference between dealer cost and the sales price. Dealer cost is recorded as the amount Al paid for a vehicle. In the case of trade-ins, the dealer cost recorded is Al's estimate of the vehicle's wholesale value. Prices in this industry are very much subject to negotiation. All sales negotiated by the sales staff must be approved by Al. Al feels that it is necessary to base much of his sales staff's commissions on the mark-up on the cars they sell. This reduces their incentive to squeeze Al's profit margin in order to make a sale.

Barbara Evans has served as Al's secretary and bookkeeper for 12 years. All records have been kept in manual form. However, the scale of operations has expanded substantially in recent years to the point where it has become very difficult for Barbara to keep the books up to date. Two years ago Barbara took an introductory computing course at a local community college. Since that time, she has been pressuring Al to buy a PC so that some of her work can be computerized. Recently, Al accepted a used PC with accompanying software as a trade-in. He now wants to begin computerizing his records. Barbara suggests that they begin by creating a file to record summary information about the stock of cars on the lot and sales of those cars. This information could be used to keep track of Al's inventory of vehicles. It could also calculate commissions due to each employee. Barbara believes that a database package could be used to develop this type of application. She does not feel that she

Database Cases

knows enough about database software to construct such an application. However, she does feel confident that she can operate an application of this type once it is developed. Al asks you to develop this application for him.

You begin discussions with Al and Barbara to determine the requirements for this system. Al indicates that he would like to be able to get a weekly listing of his inventory of vehicles. He'd like that listing to be sorted on the make of car so he can see if he has "too many Dodges and not enough Chevys." This information would help him decide which cars to bid on at the auto auctions he attends. Al also indicates that he'd like to be able to retrieve a list of the cars in stock of a particular make and model. This would help him respond to telephone calls from customers interested in a particular type of vehicle.

Barbara is primarily interested in being able to use the computer to compute commissions. Commissions are paid monthly and are based on the commission rates described above.

As you discuss the specifics of data collection with Barbara, you find that data about each vehicle are recorded at two distinct times. First, descriptive information is recorded at the time Al's Affordable Autos purchases a vehicle. This information includes the make, model, and year of the vehicle and its vehicle identification number. Also recorded are the date of the purchase and the price Al paid for the vehicle (dealer cost). Several other items about the vehicle are also recorded at this time, but Barbara feels that only the items described above need to be included in the database initially.

Additional information is recorded when a vehicle is sold. This information includes the sale date, the sales price, the salesperson's name, and the purchaser's name. Barbara notes that it is important to record the purchaser's name and have it print out on the report that calculates commissions because the sales staff keep track of their sales by the name of their customers and they will want to check to make sure that they get credit for all of their sales. In fact, she notes that salespersons frequently inquire about a specific sale to make sure that they have been credited for it.

Barbara and Al indicate that Barbara will be the only direct user of the system. She will enter the data, generate the reports, and pull out any ad-hoc information needed by Al and the sales staff. Barbara has some prior experience with the database package you are using and is confident that she will be able to handle these tasks.

Barbara is able to supply you with a small set of sample data for your use in developing this application. The sample data have been selected from cars sold over the past six weeks and cars currently in inventory, and are shown below.

Al's Sales and Inventory Sample Data

Make	Model	Year	Vehicle ID Number	Purchase Date	Dealer Cost	Sales Date	Salesp. Name	Customer Name	Sales Price
Chevy	Nova	1985	1632178153	09/06/96	675.00	10/03/93	Adams, J.	Smith R.	850.00
Pont.	Bonneville	1983	234BT82190	09/10/96	675.00	/ /			0.00
Ford	Fairlane	1979	048392X900	09/12/96	550.00	10/18/93	Davis, R.	Jones, J.	775.00
Ford	Escort	1986	007823L734	09/14/96	1535.00	/ /			0.00
Buick	Regal	1984	2183J92340	09/14/96	1175.00	10/15/93	Davis, R.	Fox, T.	1500.00
Pont.	Bonneville	1986	318BT64910	09/15/96	1850.00	/ /			0.00
Chevy	Nova	1982	0936124614	09/17/96	475.00	09/24/93	Adams, J.	Thomas, R.	650.00
Honda	Civic	1983	273812734	09/18/96	950.00	10/08/93	Lewis, L.	Robb, J.	1225.00
Dodge	Colt	1981	33J8294795	09/18/96	375.00	/ /			0.00
Ford	Escort	1986	002386X842	09/21/96	1125.00	10/24/93	Davis, R.	Owens, P.	1600.00
Pont.	Bonneville	1984	279BT28639	09/21/96	1425.00	10/19/93	Lewis, L.	Fell, R.	1675.00
Ford	Fairlane	1981	062418X237	09/26/96	800.00	/ /			0.00
Dodge	Colt	1986	64J3972905	09/26/96	1050.00	10/08/93	Adams, J.	Wells, D.	1300.00
Ford	Escort	1987	018495L273	09/28/96	2200.00	/ /			0.00
Honda	Civic	1985	392734601	09/28/96	1450.00	/ /			0.00
Chevy	Nova	1980	3897247307	09/30/96	450.00	10/19/93	Adams, J.	Morris, V.	600.00
Dodge	Colt	1984	53J9357921	10/02/96	800.00	/ /			0.00
Ford	Fairlane	1977	2846926389	10/04/96	300.00	10/27/93	Lewis, L.	Baker, H.	420.00
Honda	Civic	1983	307924783	10/06/96	1000.00	10/28/93	Davis, R.	Dowd, P.	1265.00
Dodge	Colt	1985	58J8395725	10/11/96	950.00	/ /			0.00

Database Cases

Application Development Notes

Analysis and design documents for this application are shown below. After reviewing these documents, your first step in development of this application should be to create a table documenting the structure indicated in the data dictionary form. Because the creation of the database table structure is a part of your assignment, no computerized data file is provided for this assignment. After you have created your database file, you should populate it with the sample data. The indexes required to sort the data for reporting must be created and maintained before the reports are produced. Finally the required reports should be created and tested, incorporating the calculations and summary operations described in the layout form.

Assignment

1. Based upon the data supplied and the analysis and design reports and forms provided below, develop a database application to fulfill all of the requirements of this case. Test your application for accuracy and completeness. Produce a set of printed reports based upon your sample data.

2. Write an appropriate set of documentation to accompany your application. Be sure that your documentation will fully describe all of the procedures Barbara needs to follow including procedures for control and security of the database.

3. To ensure that your application can accommodate the kinds of ad-hoc queries that are likely to be needed, execute the following queries based on your sample data:
   A. Retrieve a list of all Chevy Nova's that are in Al's inventory,
   B. Retrieve all available information about the car sold to "Fox, T.",
   C. Retrieve the total dealer cost for all vehicles in Al's inventory whose make is Chevy.

4. **MULTIPLE TABLE STRUCTURE**: Instead of the commission rates described on a previous page, assume that Al's commissions are negotiated with each salesperson and depend upon how long that salesperson has worked for Al. The current commission rates for each salesperson are:

Salesperson Name	Commission Rate Structure	
	% of Sales Price	% of Markup
Adams, J.	1.5%	8%
Davis, R.	2.0%	10%
Lewis, L.	2.0%	15%

Create a separate SALESPERSON table to store this data and generate the monthly commission report like the one shown below, but based upon data from this table linked with the INV_SALE table.

Database Cases

Application Requirements Report

OUTPUT REQUIREMENTS

1. A report of inventory of cars sorted by model is to be produced weekly.

2. A report of sales commissions is to be produced monthly. This report must show data for each sale made by a salesperson as well as a total commission earned for the month for each salesperson.

3. Support should be provided for ad-hoc retrievals of data about cars in inventory meeting selected characteristics or data about recently sold cars meeting selected characteristics. Selections are likely to be based on Make, Model, or Year of car or upon the salesperson or customer name for vehicles that have been sold.

INPUT REQUIREMENTS

All input data are to be recorded by Barbara Evans. Inventory information will be recorded at the time a car is purchased by Al's Affordable Autos. Sales information will be recorded as each vehicle is sold.

PROCESSING REQUIREMENTS

Required processing for report 1 includes selecting vehicles that have not yet been sold and sorting on Model type.

Required processing for report 2 includes selecting data for vehicles sold in the correct month, sorting and grouping data by salesperson, and calculating the commission earned for each sale and total commission earned by each salesperson.

STORAGE REQUIREMENTS

Input data are to be collected as cars are purchased and updated as each car is sold. Data will be stored for periodic reporting. Data on vehicles sold will be kept in the database until at least 60 days after the sale date.

CONTROL / USER INTERFACE REQUIREMENTS

All database operations (data entry, data correction and deletion, report generation, database querying, and back-up of the database) are to be performed exclusively by Barbara Evans.

A back-up copy of the inventory and sales file is to be made by Barbara Evans at the close of each work day.

Data Dictionary Form

TABLE NAME: INV_SALE

REQUIRED CONTROLS FOR ACCESS AND USE:

All database operations are to be performed only by Barbara Evans. When Barbara is not available, transaction information will be recorded in paper form only and entered in computerized form on Barbara's return. A backup copy of the database file is to be made just prior to the close of business each day. Data for sold vehicles are to be retained for at least 60 days after the sale date.

Column Name	Column Description	Data Type and Length	Indexed?
Make	Vehicle manufacturer, a name or abbreviation	Character 6	No
Model	Vehicle model type	Character 12	Yes nonunique
Year	Model year when the vehicle was manufactured	Character 4	No
Veh_ID	Vehicle identification number	Character 12	Yes unique
Purch_Date	Date this vehicle was purchased by Al's Affordable Autos	Date	No
Dlr_Cost	Dealer cost of vehicle	Numeric 7,2	No
Sales_Date	Date this vehicle was sold	Date	No
Slsp_Name	Name of salesperson selling this vehicle	Character 10	Yes nonunique
Cust_Name	Name of purchaser of this vehicle	Character 15	No
Sls_Price	Price for which this vehicle was sold (excluding title and taxes)	Numeric 7,2	No

Database Cases   113

Layout Forms

Inventory Report

    Input Data to   Selected data from INV_SALE for vehicles not yet
    the Report: sold (SALES_PRICE < 1) sorted by Model

Al's Affordable Autos Used Vehicle Inventory

Make	Model	Model Year	Vehicle Id Number	Date Purchased	Dealer Cost
Pont.	Bonneville	1983	M18734LV27	09/10/96	675.00
Pont.	Bonneville	1986	R19268Mr18	09/15/96	1850.00

(data from the appropriate column sorted in alphabetical order by model)

Total   (col. tot.)

Sales Commission Report

    Input data to   Selected data from INV_SALE for vehicles sold in
    the Report: the target month sorted by salesperson name

Monthly Commission Report

Make	Model	Model Year	Customer Name	Date Sold	Dealer Cost	Sales Price	Commission Earned

Salesperson: Adams, J.   ⎯ 1st value of salesp. name

| Chevy | Nova | 1985 | Smith, R. | 10/03/96 | 675.00 | 850.00 | 34.50 |

(data from the appropriate column of the INV_SALE database for this salesperson)   computed field *

Subtotal   col. sub total

Salesperson: Xxxxx, X.   ⎯ next value of salesperson name

.   .   .   .

Total   gr. tot. of col.

    *   computed commission field = sales price * .02 +
          (sales price - dealer cost) * .1

CASE 4: Knotty Pine Corporation

The Knotty Pine Corporation is a manufacturer of pine furniture. Knotty Pine sells its products to furniture wholesalers and retailers. Knotty Pine distributes a catalog describing its products to furniture wholesalers and retailers throughout the Southeastern United States and they can place orders either through the mail or over the phone, based on the catalog information.

Knotty Pine's sales are almost exclusively on a charge basis. That is, an order is filled and a bill for payment is shipped along with the order. Bills are due 30 days from the date of shipment. To encourage rapid payment of bills, Knotty Pine offers a two percent discount on all orders whose billings are paid prior to the due date. Billings which are not paid within 30 days after the due date (within 60 days of the shipment date) are considered delinquent. An interest charge of two percent per month is charged on these bills. Bills not paid within 90 days of the due date are referred to a collection agency.

Robert Henderson is head of the Accounts Receivable Department at Knotty Pine Corporation. He feels that it is very important that he keep abreast of trends in the levels of sales, receivables, and flows of payments. Mr. Henderson receives a monthly Receivables and Payments Report which includes totals for key sales, receivables, and flow of payments variables. The summary portion of this report is shown below.

```
         Receivables and Payments Report: Summary Section

Total Monthly Sales:                                    $8,239,654

Total Accounts Receivable:                              $9,154,268
     Receivables over 30 days delinquent:               $1,875,254
     Receivables over 90 days delinquent:               $  573,952

Total Payments Received:                                $8,482,390
     Discount Qualified Payments:                       $4,573,276
        (Paid within 30 days of billing)
```

Database Cases 115

The Receivables and Payments Report shows the current status of several key variables, but does not provide time trends. Mr. Henderson would like to have monthly reports and graphs displaying trends in these variables. He would also like to have the data for these variables readily available to him on his PC so that he can perform ad-hoc analysis when necessary.

The amount of data required to meet Mr. Henderson's needs is quite small. The data that is required is in aggregate form and is not considered to be sensitive or subject to restricted access. Also, the IS department at Knotty Pine Corporation has a substantial application backlog. For all of these reasons, Mr. Henderson believes that an application to meet these needs can and should be developed within his department, rather than referring it to the IS department for development.

Mr. Henderson is an experienced user of spreadsheet and database software. However, his schedule does not permit him to develop this application personally. He asks you to develop it for him. He indicates that he wants this application to store the summary information from the Receivables and Payments Report each month. He also wants a standard report and a standard set of graphs based on this data to be produced each month.

As you discuss the particulars of the application with Mr. Henderson, You find that he wants a report that tracks a set of ratios over time. The ratios he wants to track are: the ratio of accounts receivable to monthly sales, the ratio of receivables over 30 days delinquent to total accounts receivable, the ratio or receivables over 90 days delinquent to total receivables, and the ratio of discount qualified payments to total payments received. The report should show a chronological history of these ratios for at least the past year.

In addition to this report, Mr. Henderson wants to have three graphs produced each month. Each graph should plot the dollar values of a set of variables over time. The first graph should plot trends in three variables: total monthly sales, total accounts receivable, and total payments received. The second graph should plot total accounts receivable, receivables over 30 days delinquent, and receivables over 90 days delinquent. The final graph should plot total payments received and discount qualified payments. Hr. Henderson wants to see trends over the past nine months for each of these variables.

Mr. Henderson provides you with the set of summary data from the Receivables and Payments Reports shown below. He asks that you store this data in a database file so that he can easily retrieve selected data on an ad-hoc basis, and use it to develop the application that he has described.

Receivables and Payments Reports Sample Data

Time Period	Total Monthly Sales	Total	Over 30 Days Delinquent	Over 90 Days Delinquent	Total	Discount Qualified Payments
9507	7766230	7898308	1270704	335343	7826283	4044900
9508	7751181	7808742	1423528	381004	7741752	3950295
9509	7811843	7892983	1474535	313772	7702026	4362519
9510	7868606	8147357	1314853	295508	8002359	4508695
9511	7967561	8300564	1360822	319656	7927929	4364576
9512	7948906	8439276	1644570	422066	8127665	4483760
9601	7894632	8475714	1588708	455139	7989950	4425769
9602	7924156	8522969	1610258	400941	7889901	4468905
9603	8025401	8764821	1677328	422281	7896509	4316485
9604	7985609	8904719	1648633	429207	8192229	4398915
9605	8116876	9023577	1818315	526159	7892794	4393262
9606	8239654	9154268	1875254	573952	8482390	4573276

Application Development Notes

Design aids for this application are presented below, and should be carefully reviewed before as you proceed to implement this application. Your first step in implementing this application should be to create a database table implementing the structure described in the data dictionary form. When that is completed you will need to enter the set of sample data shown above. Once the database table has been created and populated, the report showing trends in key ratios must be produced. This report can be created as a database report using a set of computed fields to generate the ratios as shown in the layout forms below.

The graphs that are required for this application are not supported by many PC database packages. Unless your database package allows you to easily create graphs,

Database Cases 117

you should copy the data for the nine most recent periods into a spreadsheet file. The copied data then become the input area for a spreadsheet application that produces the requested graphs. The layout forms below assume that this procedure is to be followed.

Assignment

1. Based upon the data supplied and the analysis and design reports and forms provided below, develop an integrated application to fulfill all of the requirements of the case. Test your application for accuracy and completeness. Produce a set of printed reports based upon your sample data.

2. Write an appropriate set of documentation to accompany your application. Be sure that your documentation fully describes all of the procedures that Mr. Henderson needs to follow in operating and maintaining this application.

3. The reporting requirements of this case could have been fulfilled by developing the entire application using spreadsheet software. Write a short report discussing the advantages and disadvantages of integrated development versus spreadsheet only development for this application.

Application Requirements Report

OUTPUT REQUIREMENTS

1. Report of trends of key receivables and payments ratios covering a time period of at least 1 year and produced monthly.

2. Graphs of trends in: a) sales, receivables, and payments totals, b) receivables - total, 30 days delinquent, and 90 days delinquent, and c) payments received - total and discount qualifying. each graph is to cover a 9 month time period.

3. Support for ad-hoc queries on sales, receivables, and payments aggregates.

INPUT REQUIREMENTS

All input data are to come from monthly Receivables and Payments Reports. Data will be input on a monthly basis.

PROCESSING REQUIREMENTS

Division of variables by each other appropriately to produce ratios for reporting (1).

Conversion of data to graphical form (2).

STORAGE REQUIREMENTS

Data will be stored on a monthly basis as each month's data becomes available. Data will be retained indefinitely for reporting and retrieval purposes. Data should be saved on back-up files on a monthly basis.

CONTROL / USER INTERFACE REQUIREMENTS

All aspects of this application will be operated by Mr. Henderson who is experienced in the use of spreadsheet and database software. No sensitive or restricted data are used by this application.

Database Cases

Data Dictionary Form

TABLE NAME: REC_PMT

REQUIRED CONTROLS FOR ACCESS AND USE:

Only the head of the Accounts Receivable Department will operate this database file. A back-up copy of the file is to be made on a monthly basis after the record for the latest month has been entered and verified.

Column Name	Column Description	Data Type and Length	Indexed?
Period	Year and month of this observation expressed in 4 digits as YYMM, e.g., 9206 represents the sixth month (June) of 1992	Character 4	Yes unique
Sales	Total dollar value of sales during the month indicated	Numeric 10,0	No
Acc_Rec	Total dollar amount of accounts receivable at the end of the period	Numeric 10,0	No
Rec_Del30	Dollar amount of receivables more than 30 days delinquent at the end of the period	Numeric 10,0	No
Rec_Del90	Dollar amount of receivables more than 90 days delinquent at the end of the period	Numeric 10,0	No
Pmts_Rec	Dollar value of payments received during the month indicated	Numeric 10,0	No
Disc_Pmts	Dollar value of payments received during the month indicated which qualified for the prompt payment discount	Numeric 10,0	No

Layout Forms

Receivables and Payments Ratios Report

    Input Data to   Selected data from REC_PMT for the most recent 1
      the Report: year period sorted in ascending order by Period

Receivables and Payments Ratios

Period	Accounts Receivable to Sales Ratio	30 Day Delinquent Receivables Ratio	90 Day Delinquent Receivables Ratio	Discounted (Prompt) Payments Ratio
9507	1.267	0.203	0.061	0.573
data from period column	computed field = Acc_Rec / Sales	computed field = Rec_Del30 / Acc_Rec	computed field = Rec_Del90 / Acc_Rec	computed field = Disc_Pmts / Pmts_Rec
9606	9.999	9.999	9.999	9.999

Spreadsheet Input Data Area

```
PERIOD    SALES      ACC_REC    REC_DEL30   REC_DEL90   PMTS_REC    DISC_PMTS
9510      7385254    8261349    1769375     530278      7620961     4372901

  (Data for all variables indicated for the 9 most recent months
   available. This input data area is produced by copying
   the appropriate data from the database file REC_PMT.DBF to
   spreadsheet format.)

9606      9999999    9999999    9999999     999999      9999999     9999999
```

Graph Layouts

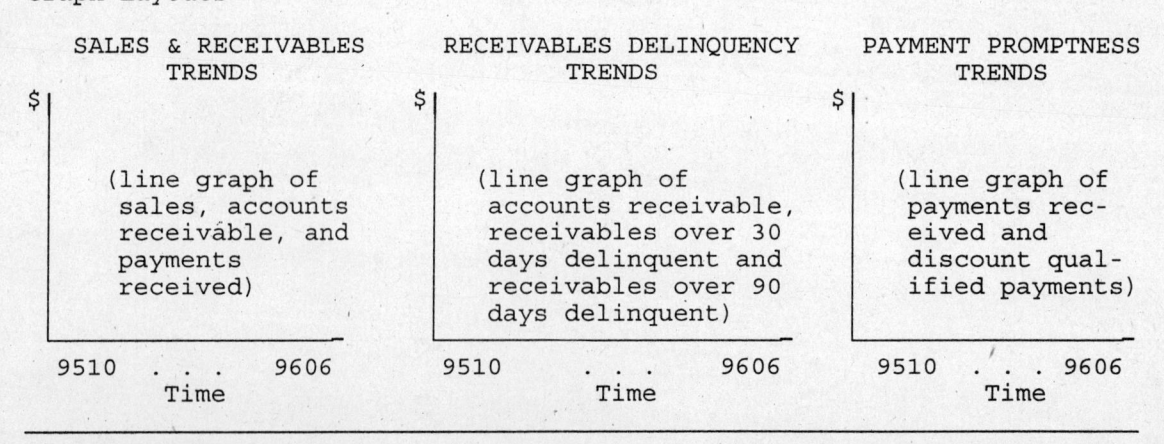

SALES & RECEIVABLES TRENDS	RECEIVABLES DELINQUENCY TRENDS	PAYMENT PROMPTNESS TRENDS
$ (line graph of sales, accounts receivable, and payments received)	$ (line graph of accounts receivable, receivables over 30 days delinquent and receivables over 90 days delinquent)	$ (line graph of payments received and discount qualified payments)
9510 . . . 9606 Time	9510 . . . 9606 Time	9510 . . . 9606 Time

Database Cases   121

CASE 5: Currier Cams

NOTE: This case is very similar to spreadsheet case 5. Here we create an integrated application to meet the requirements of the case. Data are collected and stored in a database. The database data are copied to a spreadsheet file when calculations not supported by database packages are required.

Alan Blackbridge is foreman of the Cam Assembly Department at Currier Company. His department assembles a standard cam which is used as a component in a number of Currier products. Employees in Alan's department are paid an hourly amount plus 7 cents per unit produced. The Cam Assembly Department operates 3 shifts 5 days a week, and employs 8 production workers on each shift.

An inspector randomly inspects 50 units produced by each employee each night and records the number of defective units found. The inspector also records the number of hours worked and the total number of units produced by each employee at the end of each shift. The inspector for each shift turns in a Daily Production Slip.

At the end of each week, Alicia Adams, Alan's secretary, must tabulate the total number of units produced by each employee and the number of defective units that were found. These weekly totals are recorded on an Hours and Production Report which must be sent to the Accounting department. The accounting department converts this weekly data into computerized form and uses it to process payroll and produce management reports. One of these management report is the Production Trends Report which is sent to each department's foreman on a weekly basis. Samples of the Daily Production Slip, the Hours and Production Report, and a Production Trends Report are shown below.

Alan has become concerned by a decline in the productivity of his department over the last several weeks. Alan's own observation and conversation with shift supervisors have lead him to suspect that there may be problems of absenteeism and

Sample Documents from Currier Company Cams Department

Daily Production Slip

Inspector:
Shift:
Date:

Employee Name	Emp. Id#	Hours Worked	Units Assembled	Rejected Units

---

Hours and Production Report
Department: Cam Assembly
Week of (Monday): 10/07/96

Employee Name	Emp. Id#	Hours Worked	Units Assembled	Rejected Units
J. Adams	2425	40.0	5637	17
A. Jones	3196	34.5	4732	13
B. Davis	4361	40.0	5391	11
.	.	.	.	.

Production Trends Report
Cam Assembly Department   Week of: 10/07/96

	Latest Week	Average Last 4 Weeks	Year to Date	Latest Week as % of Last 4 Weeks Avg.	Latest Week as % of Year to Date Avg
Units Assembled:	611322	623593	642805	98.0%	95.1%
% of Units Rejected:	4.7%	4.6%	4.1%	102.2%	113.3%

Database Cases 123

low productivity on certain shifts on certain days of the week. He also feels that the posting of summaries of the productivity of each shift on a weekly basis might generate a healthy competition between the shifts which could improve morale and output.

A personal computer has been installed in Alan's office. He has acquired an introductory level of knowledge in the use of a spreadsheet package and a database package. His secretary, Alicia, has learned just enough about these packages to key in data.

Alan believes that he needs an application that will do the following things:

1. record production information for each individual worker on a daily basis,

2. produce a summary report which can be used to compare performance across shifts and days of the week on a weekly basis,

3. automatically total the production information for each employee at week's end and produce the Hours and Production Report that must be sent to the accounting department.

Alan began working on this application several weeks ago. He got as far as creating a database file and has had Alicia enter the data for the most recent week into that file. However, Alan believes that he does not have the time or the skills needed to complete this application. He has asked you to complete the design and development of this application for him. If you are successful, he plans to use this application every week. He will have Alicia input the daily production data, while Alan himself plans to print out the weekly reports.

Application Development Notes

A sample of the set of data covering the most recently completed week is shown below. The full set of data for this week is available in the form of a DBASE database file called **curdata.dbf** on your data disk. An ACCESS database called **currier.mdb** is also available on your data disk. Also shown below are:

Sample Hours and Production Data

Employee Name	Emp. ID#	Shift	Week	Monday Hours Worked	Units Prod.	Reject Units	Tuesday Hours Worked	Units Prod.	...
J. Adams	2425	Day	10/07/96	8	1053	7	8	1126	...
A. Jones	3196	Day	10/07/96	8	964	4	8	1148	...
B. Davis	4361	Day	10/07/96	8	968	3	8	1077	...
C. Evans	4722	Day	10/07/96	8	1017	5	8	1175	...
T. Date	5314	Day	10/07/96	8	1019	2	8	1113	...
R. Rand	5408	Day	10/07/96	8	1054	0	8	1160	...
L. Baker	6815	Day	10/07/96	8	1045	3	8	1057	...
V. Lewis	7312	Day	10/07/96	8	1073	3	8	1066	...
B. Burt	1732	Eve.	10/07/96	8	1134	2	8	1090	...
J. Bates	2073	Eve.	10/07/96	8	1127	0	8	1110	...

an application requirements report, a diagram of the major components of this application, a data dictionary form, and a set of layout forms. Note that there are several components to this application. Data are to be stored in a database file. The weekly hours and production report to the accounts receivable department can be generated as a report file using database software. However, the report comparing performance across shifts and days requires calculations that cannot be handled by PC-based database packages (the computation of comparisons to an average). Thus, data from the database file are copied to spreadsheet format. The copied data serves as the input area for a spreadsheet application that produces the performance comparison report.

Assignment

1. Using the database file and analysis and design documents provided, develop an integrated application to meet Alan Blackbridge's requirements as described above. Be sure to test your application for accuracy and completeness. Add a documentation section to the spreadsheet portion of your application to make it as self-documenting as possible.

2. Write an appropriate set of documentation to accompany your application. Be sure that your documentation fully describes all of the procedures needed to operate the application.

3. Is the problem described in this case better handled as an integrated application

Database Cases

or by using spreadsheet software alone? Write a short paper discussing the advantages and disadvantages of alternative ways of handling this application.

4. **MULTIPLE TABLE STRUCTURE:** Assume that Alan has decided that he wants to maintain this set of production data in a form that will allow data for different weeks to be stored together in the same table. To accomplish this he will add a **Week** column to the set of fields described for the CURDATA table. At the same time, the Emp_Name and Shift fields are to be removed from this table and placed in an EMPLOYEE table since the values of these fields do not change from week to week. Emp_ID will be a field in both tables and will be used to link them together. (Emp_ID is a unique identifying field in the EMPLOYEE table.)

    The data needed to support this application are available on your data disk. there are two DBASE data files - the Employee data are in a file named **curemp.dbf** and the production week data are in a file named **curprod.dbf**. An ACCESS version of the needed set of data is available in a file named **currierm.mdb**.

    After examining these tables to ensure that you understand their structure, add any necessary indexes. Then develop an application which will allow Alan to produce the reports like those described for the single table version of this project. However, these reports should be modified so that they present summary information for all of the weeks of production information. That is, all of the production information for each employee will be summed over each week that the employee worked.

5. **MULTIPLE TABLE STRUCTURE:** In creating the Employee table, as described in part 4, we assumed that each employee will always be assigned to the same shift. Assume that employees can move between shifts, what problems could that cause given the table structure we created in part 4? How could these problems be addressed?

Application Requirements Report

OUTPUT REQUIREMENTS

1. Weekly totals of hours worked, units produced, and reject units for each worker to be submitted to the accounting department.

2. Summary report of performance by day and by shift produced weekly for distribution and analysis.

INPUT REQUIREMENTS

All input data to come from daily production slips submitted by inspectors. Data will be input on a daily basis.

PROCESSING REQUIREMENTS

Summarization of individual data to produce weekly totals by worker for hours, production, and reject units (1).

Summarization of data to produce averages and comparisons to average by shift and by day (2).

STORAGE REQUIREMENTS

Data have no immediate use in other applications. Data will be saved on backup files on a weekly basis for possible future use.

CONTROL / USER INTERFACE REQUIREMENTS

Individual worker performance data are sensitive and should be available only to those who need to know. A backup copy of the data should be made each week when data entry has been completed and checked.

The data entry portion of the application will be accessed on a repeated basis by a novice user. The remaining portions of the application will be operated by a user with intermediate level computer skills.

Database Cases

Partial Data Dictionary Form

TABLE NAME: CURDATA

REQUIRED CONTROLS FOR ACCESS AND USE:

Only the foreman and his secretary are to have access to this database file. The secretary is to perform data entry tasks only. A back-up copy of this file is to be made at the close of each week, after data have been verified but before any reporting or analysis functions are performed.

Column Name	Column Description	Data Type and Length	Indexed?
Emp_Name	Name of employee stored as first initial and last name, e.g., J. Smith	Character 10	No
Emp_ID	ID number of employee, a unique 4 digit number	Character 4	Yes, with Week Unique
Shift	Shift this worker is assigned to Day, Eve., or Ngt.	Character 4	No
Week	Date of the first day of this work week	Date	Yes, with Emp_ID Unique
Mon_Hrs	Hours worked on Monday	Numeric 4.1	No
Mon_Prod	Units produced on Monday	Numeric 5	No
Mon_Rej	Number of reject units produced on Monday	Numeric 3	No

. (The same three fields Hrs, Prod, and Rej are specified
. for the remainder of the week - Tue, Wed, Thu, and Fri)

Application Components for Integrated Implementation

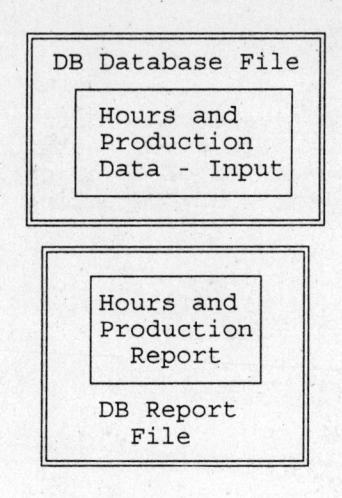

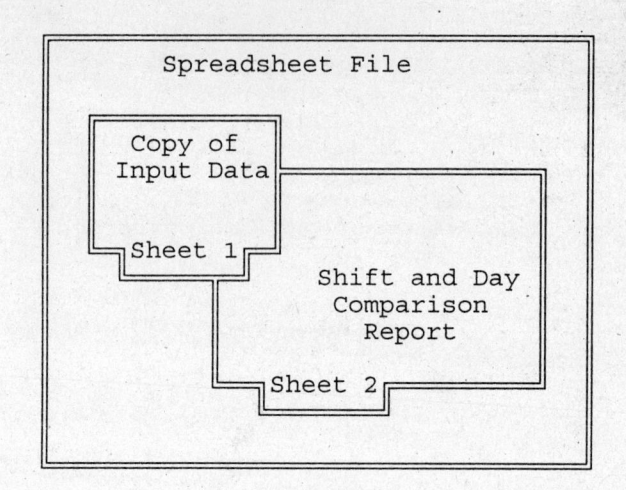

```
┌─────────────────────────┐      ┌──────────────────────────────────┐
│  DB Database File       │      │  Spreadsheet File                │
│   ┌─────────────────┐   │      │   ┌──────────────┐               │
│   │ Hours and       │   │      │   │ Copy of      │               │
│   │ Production      │   │      │   │ Input Data   │               │
│   │ Data - Input    │   │      │   │              │               │
│   └─────────────────┘   │      │   │     Sheet 1  │               │
└─────────────────────────┘      │   └──────┬───────┴──────────┐    │
                                 │          │ Shift and Day    │    │
┌─────────────────────────┐      │          │ Comparison       │    │
│   ┌─────────────────┐   │      │          │ Report           │    │
│   │ Hours and       │   │      │          │                  │    │
│   │ Production      │   │      │          │         Sheet 2  │    │
│   │ Report          │   │      │          └──────────────────┘    │
│   └─────────────────┘   │      └──────────────────────────────────┘
│   DB Report             │
│   File                  │
└─────────────────────────┘
```

Layout Forms

Weekly Hours and Production Report

    Input data to
        the Report: Selected data from CURDATA for the current week.

    Weekly Hours and Production by Worker

Employee Name	Emp. ID#	Hours Worked	Units Produced	Reject Units
J. Adams 1234 XXXXXXX 9999 . (names and ID# fields from the database file) XXXXXXX 9999		40.0 99.9 (computed field, sum of Mon_Hrs through Fri_Hrs) 99.9	4873 99999 (computed field sum of Mon_Prod through Fri_Prod) 99999	12 999 (computed field sum of Mon_Rej through Fri_Rej) 999

Database Cases

Spreadsheet Input Area: Daily Hours and Production Data

```
EMP_NAME   SHIFT WEEK     MON_HRS MON_PROD MON_REJ TUE_HRS TUE_PROD ..
J. Adams   Day   10/07/96   8.0     1053      7      8.0     1126

   (Data for all days of the week for all three shifts for the
   week indicated. This spreadsheet data area is to be produced
   by copying the appropriate data from the database file CURDATA.DBF
   to spreadsheet format. The spreadsheet file created provides the
   data for this input area.)

X. Xxxxx   Ngt.  10/07/96   9.9     9999      9      9.9     9999  ..
```

Shift and Day Comparison Report Area:

                Summary Shift and Day Comparison Report

                   Mon.   Tue.   Wed.   Thur.   Fri.   Week-to-date
Units Produced

```
  Day Shift       99999   99999   99999   99999   99999    99999
  Evening Shift   (sum of units produced by shift on day   (sum of daily
  Night Shift      from cells in the input data area)       shift tots.)

  Average         (         average across the three shifts            )
```

% of Average Units Produced

```
  Day Shift       999.9% 999.9%  . . .                     999.9%
  Evening Shift   (         shift value divided by average        )
  Night Shift       .       .       .       .       .        .
```

Reject Units

```
  Day Shift         999     999     999     999     999     9999
  Evening Shift   (sum of reject units by shift on day    (sum of daily
  Night Shift      from cells in the input data area)      shift tots.)

  Average         (         average across the three shifts            )
```

% of Average Reject Units

```
  Day Shift       999.9% 999.9%  . . .                     999.9%
  Evening Shift   (         shift value divided by average        )
  Night Shift       .       .       .       .       .        .
```

CASE 6: Teen Temps

Teen Temps is a nonprofit employment agency which attempts to place teenagers in temporary jobs during the summer vacation period. Teen Temps operates in a city with a population of about 50,000 located in the Southeastern United States. Teen Temps specializes in placing students in temporary jobs whose duration ranges from a few hours to two weeks. Students wishing to be employed can sign up with Teen Temps by coming in and filling out a form. No fee is charged to the student workers. People or organizations wishing to hire a teenager do pay a small fee. For this fee, they can receive a list of available teenagers with the skills they need. Alternatively, the prospective employer can request that Teen Temps select a worker for them. In the former case, the employer selects the worker they want and then informs Teen Temps of who they selected and the date that the job will be completed. In the latter case, the staff of Teen Temps contacts qualified teenagers until they find one who is available for the requested job.

Thus far, all data about the teen workers has been kept on index cards. As each job comes, in the cards are searched to find potential qualified workers. There are substantial problems with this method of record keeping. First, searching records manually is very awkward and time consuming. Secondly, it is difficult to keep track of how often a particular teenager is offered employment. Last summer there were numerous complaints that some teens were called for jobs much less frequently than others "with the same sets of skills." Finally, the manual system simply is not capable of handling the volume of teen workers and jobs expected for the coming summer. The program has proven to be very successful over the previous two years and substantial growth is expected for the coming summer.

Teen Temps' is about to begin its third summer of operation. Nicky James has worked as a volunteer on the teen temp's staff for the previous two years and has been selected to manage operations this summer. One of her highest priorities is to computerize the data about teen workers that is maintained. Teen Temps has a PC with database software available to it for the summer. You have volunteered some time to help get the teen temps program going this year and, knowing that you have experience with PC software, Nicky has asked you to develop this application.

Database Cases

Nicky is able to supply you with a sample of the index cards used to record worker information last year. One of these cards is shown below.

```
              Sample Teen Worker Index Card

    NAME:     Ann Carnes
    PHONE#:   638-2174

    TIMES AVAILABLE:
      days and evenings, no weekends

    JOBS/SKILLS:
      babysitting, yard work
```

From her experience over the past two summers, Nicky feels that she can identify the key characteristics of teen workers that potential employers need to know. These include: is this worker available for evening work? for weekend work? What skills do they possess and what types of work are they willing to do? Specifically, there are three important characteristics: is the worker willing and able to do babysitting, is the worker willing and able to do heavy physical jobs, such as yard work, and finally is the worker willing and able to do housekeeping jobs.

Another issue that Nicky raises with you is fairness in allocating workers to jobs. She wants to have a system that will ensure that all teens have the same opportunity to secure jobs through the system. Toward this end, she suggests that a contact date be stored in the database. This date would be updated each time a worker is contacted about a job opportunity. Nicky is hoping that this date can be used to sort the list of teen workers retrieved for any job assignment, so that those who have gone the longest since the last job opportunity will be placed at the top of the list and contacted first. Once a teen worker is contacted about a job this "contact date" would be updated whether or not they took the job. Some teen workers are much more flexible about the types of work they are willing to do and the times they are willing to do it, and Nicky feels that those workers should be rewarded. However, when a prospective employer requests a list of available workers, only the worker selected should have the contact date on their record updated. This is because Teen Temps has no way of knowing which of the teens on the prospect list were actually contacted.

Under the manual index card system, the cards of teens placed in jobs were pulled from the active file and placed in a file of unavailable workers organized by the concluding date of the job assignment. At the end of each day, the cards for workers whose jobs were scheduled to end on that day were returned to the active file. Nicky indicates that your application will need to do something of this nature. That is, you will need to know which teen workers are assigned to jobs that are not yet completed and will have to ensure that those workers are not included in lists of prospective workers for jobs with overlapping dates. Nicky suggests that this might be accomplished by storing the completion date for a job in the record for the worker who is assigned to that job. A history of job assignments will not be needed, but simply a record of the completion date of the last job assigned to a worker. This would be updated each time a worker takes a new job assignment.

The application you create should be able to produce a report listing the names and phone numbers of teen workers available for a particular job. This report should be sorted on "contact date" so that the worker with the least recent contact will be placed at the top of the list. To be "available" for a job a worker must not have a current job whose dates overlap with the proposed job, they must have indicated that they were willing to do jobs of the type of the proposed job, and they must have indicated that they were willing to work at the times of day and week when the proposed job will occur.

A variety of volunteer workers will be retrieving listings of available workers, entering data records for new workers who have just signed up, and updating the records of teen workers who are contacted and/or accepted for new job assignments. Nicky herself will handle an ad-hoc querying of the system, making of back-up copies of the database, and correction of mistakes. Nicky James has an intermediate level of skill in the use of database packages. However, many of her volunteer workers have no previous computing experience.

To help you get a feel for the data involved, Nicky has been able to provide you with the sample set of data below. These data are for your use in developing and testing the application. She has even included a set of hypothetical contact and job completion dates for your use.

Database Cases

```
                    Sample Teen Worker Data

                                 Skills and Interests    Job       Job
Worker    Phone   Availability   Baby- House Yard      Contact    Compl.
  Name     No.   Eves.  Wkends.  Sitter work  work      Date       Date

Ann Carnes   8-2174   Yes   No     Yes   No    Yes    08/22/96   08/17/96
Dan Smith    4-6284   Yes   Yes    No    Yes   Yes    08/18/96   08/23/96
Jan Jones    8-2762   No    No     Yes   Yes   No     08/23/96   08/16/96
Pat Carnes   8-2174   Yes   Yes    Yes   Yes   Yes    08/21/96   08/22/96
Dale Boyd    6-8629   No    Yes    No    No    Yes    08/17/96   08/06/96
Jim Joyce    4-8274   Yes   Yes    Yes   No    Yes    08/23/96   08/16/96
Pam Powers   7-1037   No    No     Yes   No    No     08/16/96     /  /
Ed Flynn     4-8297   Yes   No     No    Yes   Yes    08/20/96   08/21/96
Brad Case    6-2869   Yes   Yes    Yes   Yes   Yes    08/22/96   08/21/96
Sue Taylor   7-8273   No    Yes    Yes   No    No     08/18/96   08/15/96
Stan Mann    4-8326   Yes   Yes    No    No    Yes    08/20/96   08/12/96
Alice Ames   5-8392   No    Yes    No    Yes   Yes    08/16/96   08/19/96
Lynn Cline   6-8273   Yes   Yes    Yes   Yes   Yes    08/19/96   08/24/96
Ben Barnes   6-0927   Yes   No     No    No    Yes    08/18/96   08/06/96
Della Eads   8-2132   Yes   Yes    Yes   Yes   No     08/23/96   08/25/96
```

Application Development Notes

Before beginning to implement your application for this case, you should develop an appropriate set of analysis and design aids. The design and creation of a database table structure is an important part of this case. Based on the sample data shown, you should develop a data dictionary form for the data of this application and use its specification in creating your table structure. After creating the table you will need to enter and verify the sample data that are provided. An appropriate index will need to be created and maintained to sort the data appropriately for the required reporting. The report structure for this application is quite simple, but the selection used to determine the set of workers available for a job can be quite complex. You will want to test the selection criteria very carefully.

Assignment

1. Based on the description above and the sample data shown, generate an appropriate set of analysis and design aids for this application. Using these aids, develop a database application meeting all of the requirements of this case. Test your application for accuracy and completeness.

2. Write an appropriate set of documentation to accompany your application. Be sure that your documentation fully describes all of the procedures that Nicky and her volunteer workers need to follow. Procedures should be described in a level of detail that is matched to the needs of the different users of the system. You should also be sure that your procedures include complete descriptions of control and back-up procedures to be used.

3. To ensure that your reporting system works properly, generate and print lists of available workers for the following job assignments:
    A. Someone wants a worker for an evening baby sitting job on 08/23/96
    B. Someone wants a worker to do yard work including some weekend work, and their job begins on 08/26/96
    C. Someone wants a worker to do house work during daytime hours, on a weekday, beginning on 08/23/96.

4. **MULTIPLE TABLE STRUCTURE:** Suppose that Nicky decides that she would also like to keep a list of jobs in computerized form. She wants to assign a job number to each job request as it comes in. She will also record the Name and Phone Number of the person requesting the work, the type of work, estimated hours of work, the name of the worker assigned to the job, and its completion date. Nicky wants to be able to link this job data with her data about workers to produce a report showing the job number, the employer's name and phone number and the assigned worker's name and phone number for all jobs that do not have a completion date. She also wants to produce a summary report showing the total estimated hours of work assigned to each of her teen workers.

Database Cases

Based upon this description and the sample of JOB data shown below develop a multiple table application to meet Nicky's needs.

Sample of Job Data

Job No.	Employer Name	Employer Phone #	Type of Job	Est. Hours	Assigned Worker Name	Completion Date
121	Ann Smith	3-7819	House Work	6	Jan Jones	08/10/96
128	Lee Davis	4-8136	Yard Work	8	Jim Joyce	08/12/96
133	Jack Dahl	4-2973	House Work	5	Pat carnes	/ /
137	Ali Grant	7-2193	Babysitter	4	Jan Jones	08/16/96
142	Lynn Bush	3-2851	Babysitter	3	Jim Joyce	08/14/96
155	Sue Smith	5-1890	Yard Work	16	Stan Mann	08/12/96
162	Ann Taws	7-9105	Yard Work	5	Jim Joyce	08/16/96
167	Dan Price	4-2867	House Work	10	Della Eads	/ /
176	Ed Vance	3-9217	Babysitter	4	Lynn Cline	08/24/96
181	Dee Morris	2-6193	House Work	8	Brad Case	/ /
183	Eve Cole	5-7623	Yard Work	7	Dale Boyd	/ /
188	Jan Jones	6-6832	Babysitter	5	Lynn Cline	/ /

CASE 7: Ron's Restaurant Supplies - Database

NOTE: This case is based upon the same situation described in spreadsheet case 8. This case is designed to show that many application can be developed using either spreadsheet or database software.

Ron's Restaurant Supplies is a wholesaler of restaurant supplies and equipment. The business started as a supplier of coffee and coffee equipment to restaurants. Over the years, Ron's has expanded its product lines to include a wide variety of nonperishable expendable restaurant supplies and restaurant equipment. Basically, if a restaurant needs it, and it doesn't need to be delivered in a refrigerated truck, Ron's supplies it.

The sales staff at Ron's Restaurant Supplies are paid primarily on a commission basis. Sales staff receive commissions whose amount is based on three components. A percentage commission is paid on sales of supplies, a different and higher percentage commission is paid on sales of equipment, and a bonus amount is paid for each new customer found by a salesperson. *The rates that are currently in effect are 1 percent on sales of supplies, 2 percent on sales of equipment, and a 40 dollar bonus for each new customer.*

The commission rates are set by the Vice President of Marketing, Ms. Nancy Evans. Ms. Evans likes to make adjustments to the commission rate structure occasionally to provide incentives in areas where growth has lagged. For instance, if equipment sales are running slow and equipment inventory is up, she may temporarily raise the commission percentage for equipment. Similarly, if she feels that the sales staff has not found enough new customers lately she may raise the bonus for new customers. When adjustments to the commission structure are made, they are effective at the beginning of the next calendar month.

Because of the complexity and changing nature of the commission system used, commissions have always been hand calculated. Ron's Restaurant Supplies uses

Database Cases 137

a PC based accounting software package to handle its order processing and billing. That package is used to produce a printed monthly summary which lists total sales of supplies and total sales of equipment for each salesperson. Each salesperson submits a list of new customers they have attracted that month and this is verified from the accounting data to determine the count of new customers. A listing for a typical month is shown below, and is available in the form of a DBASE database file named **ronsdata.dbf** and in an ACCESS database named **Ronsdata.mdb** on your data disk.

```
         Summary Sales Data for Ron's Restaurant Supplies


     Salesperson      Salesp.    Sales of      Sales of        New
        Name          Number     Supplies      Equipment    Customers

     Elston, Ed         101       41495         42275           0
     Barnes, John       102       50555         23006           1
     Moran, Sue         103       52704         43011           2
     Wells, Ann         104       45761         37530           4
     Thomas, Bob        105       38469         39204           0
     Sanders, Arnold    106       39071         49281           6
     Lewis, Barbara     107       53350         48864           3
     Franklin, Jim      108       44492         22549           4
     Howell, Victor     109       59228         35479           4
     Murray, Ben        110       46364         31018           5
     Peterson, Pamela   111       37089         45134           1
     Naylor, William    112       47067         36811           4
     Owens, Louis       113       41575         43400           4
     Garland, John      114       37491         29009           5
     Martinez, Phil     115       33906         48585           3
     Phelps, Brad       116       46146         24940           6
     Darnel, Darlene    117       48103         49480           5
     Hartlett, Gene     118       40793         29705           1
```

Ms. Evans has requested that you create a computer application to store this monthly listing and produce a report showing the amount of commission and bonus owed to each salesperson. She would also like to have summary information, such as totals for: sales of supplies, sales of equipment, the number of new customers, and commissions paid. There are no current plans to produce reports based upon data from prior months. However, Ms. Evans does want to retain each month's data in an accessible form for possible future uses.

Ms. Evans indicates that she has no experience with the use of computers and plans to turn the application over to her assistant, Dan Howard. Dan has experience in using word processing on the computer but is a novice in the use of spreadsheet and database software.

Application Development Notes

Since a database table specifying the structure of the data for this case has been provided, you should examine the structure of this table as you begin to design your application. An appropriate set of analysis and design documents should be created for this case. Then, using these documents and the data provided, you will proceed to create a database report to produce the required summary report. Calculation of the commission earned by each salesperson can be done through a query.

Assignment

1. Based on the description above and the database file provided, generate an appropriate set of analysis and design aids for this application. Using these aids, develop a database application meeting all the requirements of this case. Test your application for accuracy and completeness.

2. Write an appropriate set of documentation to accompany your application. Be sure that your documentation fully describes all of the procedures Dan needs to follow including appropriate back-up procedures.

3. Write a brief discussion paper addressing the following questions:
    A. What are the advantages and disadvantages of using a database package as opposed to a spreadsheet package for this application.
    B. Could you build an application using your database software package that would allow you to keep track of cumulative "year-to-date"

Database Cases 139

commissions earned by salespersons. Note that, to do this, your application would have to record the amount of commission earned by each salesman each month in the database and would need to allow commission rates to be modified without changing the value of commissions earned in previous months. Describe how you would modify your application to accomplish this task. If you feel that the task described above cannot be performed using your database package, describe the limitations of your database package that prevent you from accomplishing it.

4. **MULTIPLE TABLE STRUCTURE:** Assume that Ms. Evans has decided that she would like to retain each month's summary sales data in a table that would keep a history of sales trends over time. In addition, salespersons are paid a small salary, as well as their commission, each month. Ms. Evans would like to add the salary amount and a total gross pay calculation for each salesperson to the information in the summary sales report that was described for the single table application.

   To accommodate these changes, the structure of the sales table has been modified by adding a Sales_Month attribute and removing the Salesperson_Name attribute. The Sales_Month attribute records the beginning date of the sales month. Each salesperson has one row in this table for each month he or she works. A sample set of data for this table covering the months of January and February 1996 is provided on your data disk. This set of data is available in a DBASE database file called **ronsm.dbf** and in an ACCESS file called **ronsmsls.mdb**.

   Since the Salesperson Number can be used to identify each salesperson, the Salesperson name attribute is removed to an EMPLOYEE table. The EMPLOYEE table will have the Salesperson Number, Salesperson Name, and Salary as its attributes. The Salesperson Number will be the common attribute linking the EMPLOYEE table to the table containing monthly sales data. The set of data needed for the EMPLOYEE table is shown below:

Employee Table Data for Ron's Restaurant Supplies

Salesperson Name	Salesp. Number	Monthly Salary
Elston, Ed	101	$250
Barnes, John	102	$300
Moran, Sue	103	$325
Wells, Ann	104	$275
Thomas, Bob	105	$250
Sanders, Arnold	106	$300
Lewis, Barbara	107	$350
Franklin, Jim	108	$275
Howell, Victor	109	$300
Murray, Ben	110	$250
Peterson, Pamela	111	$275
Naylor, William	112	$325
Owens, Louis	113	$300
Garland, John	114	$275
Martinez, Phil	115	$250
Phelps, Brad	116	$300
Darnel, Darlene	117	$325
Hartlett, Gene	118	$300

Create an appropriate table structure for this set of employee data and add the set of data shown. Then build an application that will provide the summary sales, commission, and gross pay information described above for any month.

5. **MULTIPLE TABLE STRUCTURE:** Modify the application you developed in part 4 to include report that summarizes year-to-date sales and pay information for each employee.

CASE 8: Kwik Shop Movie Rentals

The Kwik Shop is a convenience store located in a small resort area. Because of its remote location, the Kwik Shop stocks not only convenience foods, but also a variety of hardware and houseware supplies. Lucy Davis, owner of the Kwik Shop, has always attempted to expand the services her shop offers in response to changing markets.

Two years ago, Lucy began offering VCR rentals. Memberships are available at no charge to area residents. Lucy has about 100 members of her video club and maintains an inventory of about 150 movies. Until now, she has maintained all video club records in manual form. She has purchased a personal computer and would like to automate much of her record keeping, beginning with her video rental operations.

Lucy has assigned each club member a unique three digit member ID number. Each membership is in essence a family membership, so that all family members can rent a movie using one common member ID number. Lucy has an index card for each membership showing the member ID number, the member's name, address, and phone number, and a list of names of additional family members who are permitted to rent movies under this membership. She keeps this set of index cards stored in order by member ID number, so that she can quickly verify the identity of a customer.

Lucy also keeps a set of index cards describing her inventory of movies. The information she maintains for each movie lists the movie's title, the category of the movie (Family, Western, Drama, Comedy), the movie's rating (G, PG, or R), and a unique four character ID code that Lucy assigns to each movie when it is received. Samples of the cards Lucy uses are shown below.

Rentals are made strictly on a cash basis. That is, each customer pays a one-day rental fee for the videos she/he rents at the time of the rental. All movies are due to be returned by six o'clock of the evening following the date on which they are rented. Movies returned late are subject to an appropriate additional fee which is

Customer Index Card

```
CUSTOMER ID#:    073

CUSTOMER NAME:   Joe Davis

ADDRESS:         348 Lark Lane

PHONE #:         4-2843

ADDITIONAL           Susan Davis
FAMILY MEMBERS:      Janet Davis
                     Bobby Davis
```

Movie Index Card

```
MOVIE ID#:    A028

MOVIE TITLE:  Dead Again

CATEGORY:     Drama

 RATING:      PG

DATE RENTED:
```

---

collected at the time that they are returned. When a movie is rented, the rental date is written, in pencil, on that movie's index card. The index card for the movie is then placed behind the card of the member checking it out. When a movie is returned, the date on the card is checked and a late fee is charged if appropriate. Then the date is erased and the movie card is returned to its file.

The most critical aspect of managing video rentals is keeping track of the stock of video tapes. Which movies are out and which are in? Who has a particular video? Is a video overdue to be returned? Currently, Lucy retains a copy of a printed rental slip for each rental and must search through those slips to locate a particular movie.

Lucy plans to eventually computerize her entire movie rental operation. However, her most immediate concern is to improve the information she has available to manage her inventory of movies. She wants to develop a computerized system to track her inventory of movies which can interface with her manual system of member information. The member information will be computerized in a later step. As a part of her inventory tracking, she wants to keep track of the status of each movie - is it in the store or is it checked out to some customer. At this point, she is not interested in keeping a rental history for each movie she only wants to know whether it is currently checked out and, if so, who checked it out and on what date did they check it out?

Database Cases 143

Lucy has asked you to develop an application for her that will store information about her inventory of movie videos and allow her to retrieve summary information about them. Lucy would like to have your application give her the types of information described below.

1. Printed lists of movies by category. The lists should show the ID number, title, and rating for each movie and be grouped by category. These printed lists would be provided to customers to help them select movies.

2. A list of all movies that have been out for more than one day. This list would show the name and title of the movie, the customer ID number of the customer who rented it, and the date of the rental. This list would be used to assess late fees and to call customers who may have forgotten to return the movies they rented.

3. Displays of information to answer customer questions. For example, a customer might ask about the status of a movie - is it checked out, who has it, when is it due back? Also, a customer might ask to see whether there are any movies listed as checked out to them.

Lucy has prepared the set of sample data shown below for your use. This sample reflects the current status of selected movies in Lucy's inventory. For the movies that are rented, Lucy has added the ID number of the member who checked them out since she wants this data to be available in her database.

Application Development Notes

Your first step in developing the application for this case should be to perform analysis and design activities and generate an appropriate set of analysis and design aids for use in implementing your application. The design and creation of a database table structure is an important part of this case. Based on the description above and the sample data shown, you should develop a data dictionary form for this data and use its specification in creating your table. Once your table has been created, you will need to enter the sample data shown below. Before creating reports for this application, you should create any indexes needed to sort your data appropriately for use in your reports. Finally, you should create the report or reports needed to meet the output requirements of this application.

```
              Sample of Kwik Shop Movie Inventory Data

Movie                           Type of              Date    Member
 ID#    Movie Title              Movie      Rating  Rented   Id #

A023    Fantasia                 Children's   G       / /
B026    The Good, the Bad, & the Ugly  Western  PG   09/22/96  073
A015    The African Queen        Drama        G       / /
A028    Dead Again               Adventure    PG    09/21/96  058
C009    City Slickers            Comedy       PG      / /
A023    Fatal Attraction         Drama        R     09/22/96  024
B026    The Terminator           Adventure    R       / /
A043    When Harry Met Sally     Comedy       PG    09/20/96  046
A029    The Rocketeer            Adventure    PG    09/21/96  058
B003    Witness for the Prosecution  Drama    PG    09/22/96  024
C017    The Never Ending Story   Children's   G       / /
C042    The Shootist             Western      PG    09/22/96  073
B031    The Graduate             Drama        PG      / /
B006    Raiders of the Lost Ark  Adventure    PG    09/22/96  052
B024    The Grey Fox             Western      PG      / /
C014    The Man From Snowy River Western      G     09/22/96  052
A064    Hard Times               Comedy       G     09/21/96  042
B041    Children of a Lesser God Drama        PG      / /
A019    The War of the Roses     Comedy       R     09/22/96  006
C002    Dr. Strangelove          Comedy       PG      / /
```

Assignment

1. Based on the description above and the sample data shown, design a full set of analysis and design aids for this application. Using these aids, develop a database application meeting all the requirements of this case. Test your application for accuracy and completeness. Get a printed listing of all reports produced by your application.

2. Write an appropriate set of documentation to accompany your application. Be sure that your documentation fully describes all of the procedures that Lucy will need to follow including appropriate back-up procedures.

3. To test your application's capability to support a variety of ad-hoc queries, retrieve the following sets of data and get a printed listing of your results:

A. a list of all movies checked out to the customer whose ID number is 58,
B. all information in the record for the movie "When Harry Met Sally",
C. the names and numbers of all Comedy movies that are currently available.

4. **MULTIPLE TABLE STRUCTURE:** Suppose Lucy wanted to have additional information about customers listed on her report of movies that are overdue to be returned. Perhaps she would like to have the name and address of the customer listed as well as the customer ID number. A sample list of Customer information cards is shown below. The data shown are designed to match the inventory data. (The Additional Family Members attribute is not included and is discussed below.) Modify your application to support the storage and retrieval of this information.

```
              Customer Index Card Information

Customer    Customer
   ID#        Name       Address              Phone #

   073      Joe Davis    348 Lark Lane        4-2843

   058      Ann Nolan    214 Sparrow Dr.      4-2752
   024      Edie Bates   409 Lakeview Lane    3-1973
   046      Ed Ault      146 Sparrow Dr.      4-2391
   042      Ross Cass    106 Elm Trail        3-2061
   052      Sue Dean     206 Lark Lane        4-1924
   006      Al Polk      304 Elm Trail        3-1762
```

5. **MULTIPLE TABLE STRUCTURE:** Suppose Lucy wanted to store information about all family members authorized to use a given card in the database. She wants this information stored in a way that makes it easy to retrieve information about a membership based on knowing the name of any authorized user. Also suppose Lucy wants to keep a history of all rentals of each of her tapes. Write a short paper describing the set of tables you would use to support these requirements and discussing how they would be linked together.

CASE 9: Grand Grounds Incorporated

Grand Grounds is a regional processor and distributer of coffee. The coffee that Grand Grounds distributes is made from a special blend of beans using a carefully guarded process. The beans and process used by Grand Grounds are quite expensive. Thus, Grand Grounds coffees compete with upscale blended and flavored coffees. However, Grand Grounds distributes only its single original type of coffee. Grand Grounds sells its coffees primarily to supermarkets.

Grand Grounds coffee is vacuum sealed in a plastic pouch rather than being sealed in a can. Freshness is an important consideration for coffee consumers so, to insure freshness, each pound of coffee is imprinted with a sales suspension date. Coffee not sold by this date is returned to the warehouse to be given to local soup kitchens or destroyed. The suspension dating policy that Grand Grounds uses gives their product an effective shelf life of only a little over two weeks.

Patricia Stevens, Vice President of Marketing at Grand Grounds is concerned that sales and stockage information is not being used effectively enough at the supermarket level by individual salespersons. She feels that salespersons are stocking some stores too heavily leading to product having to be destroyed. Even when the suspension date is not reached, coffee on the shelves that is near its suspension date tends to discourage purchases. excessive stockage also increases Grand Grounds inventory holding costs.

An even bigger problem is the fact that some supermarkets are inadequately stocked with Grand Grounds coffees. Salespersons are often required to make emergency restocks of these stores disrupting sales routes and, more importantly, at some stores outages may occur without the Grand Grounds salesperson being notified.

Grand Grounds salespersons can reduce stockages to stores with lagging sales on their own initiative. However, stockage can be increased only with the approval of the supermarket manager. Supermarket display space is a precious resource since expanded display space tends to spur additional sales.

Ms. Stevens would like to be able to provide each salesperson with the information they need to manage their stockage more effectively. She wants to provide her sales staff with reports showing recent trends in stockage level, sales, and the rate at which the stockage (or inventory) is turned over for each store they serve. The sales staff could use these reports to cut back stockage at stores with lagging sales and to help make the case for increased display space at stores where inventory turnover is high.

The profit margin to supermarkets on the sales of Grand Grounds coffees is substantially higher than that for standard national brands. Supermarket managers tend to think of Grand Grounds as a low turnover specialty item requiring a higher profit margin and only a minimal amount of shelf space. Ms. Stevens feels that sales statistics for Grand Grounds justify increased display space in many stores. She would like to provide each salesperson with a portable PC and an application that would allow them to share information about a store's sales with that stores manager. She feels that reports and graphics presenting sales data directly to store managers in computerized form would be a particularly effective way to persuade them to expand the display space assigned to Grand Grounds. She envisions an application that would allow a store manager to see trends in sales, stockage, and the inventory turnover rate for their store. The salesperson could even access the data to do ad-hoc querying or to perform calculations to respond to specific questions a store manager might pose.

The data needed for this application are available in an organizational database maintained by the IS staff. They are able to provide the data that Ms. Stevens has in mind in the form of a database files with the standard **.dbf** file extension format that is used by DBASE and can be read by most other PC database packages. She expects the application you develop to access summary data from organizational databases maintained by Grand Grounds IS staff.

Ms. Stevens asks you to work with the IS department to get a set of sample data and use that data to build a prototype of this application system. She specifically asks that your prototype application produce a report sorted by store and summarizing recent data about sales and stockage levels. She asks that this report include a computation of the daily sales rate for each store over each sales period. She also requests that your application also include a method of extracting data about

Database Cases

individual stores for reporting and graphical presentation to the store's manager. Because store managers should not have access to data about sales by competitors, it is important that they be given access only to data for their own store. Ms. Stevens wants this portion of the application to present recent trends in sales, sales per day, stockage level, and the rate of inventory turnover.

Upon consultation with the IS department you are provided with a small sample of data for one salesperson covering a one month time period. A few records of this data are shown below and this set of sample data is available on your data disk in a DBASE database file called **grnddata.dbf**. If you are using a database package other than DBASE you will need to use the import operation to retrieve this table of data into your database.

Sample Sales and Stockage Data

Sales-person No.	Store Name	Date of Sale	Days Since Previous Sales Visit	Pounds of Coffee Sold	Pounds of Coffee Stocked
M7602	Jones' #46	08/25/93	7	280	350
M7602	Fresh - N - Rite #17	08/25/93	6	209	380
M7602	Jones' #48	08/26/93	7	325	325
M7602	Econo Bag	08/26/93	10	178	300
M7602	Vin's Supr Mart #7	08/27/93	8	343	400
M7602	Vin's Supr Mart #9	08/27/93	8	350	350
M7602	Jones' #46	09/01/93	7	298	350
M7602	Jones' #48	09/01/93	6	325	350
M7602	Fresh - N - Rite #17	09/02/93	8	236	360

Note that the number of days since the last previous sales visit has been computed from the organizational database and is included in this file. Based on this data, the daily sales rate for a store can be computed as pounds of coffee sold divided by the number of days since the previous visit. Once the daily sales rate is known, the inventory turnover rate can be calculated by dividing the pound of coffee stocked by the daily sales rate. For example, for the first record, average daily sales are 280 divided by 7 which equals 40 pounds per day. Based on that figure, the inventory turnover rate can be calculated as 350 divided by 40 which equals 8 and 3/4 days.

Application Development Notes

Since a database file specifying the structure of the data and providing a sample set of records for this case has been provided, you should examine the structure of this table as you begin to design your application. An appropriate set of analysis and design documents should be created for this case. Then, using these documents and the data provided you will proceed to create a reporting system to produce the required reports. An appropriate index should be created and maintained to sort the data in the required order for reporting. The report summarizing recent sales trends across all stores can be generated within your database package. However, the data covering sales trends for an individual store should be linked into a spreadsheet file for analysis. Converting this data to spreadsheet form will make it easy to support the graphical output that is needed. Storing the individual store data in spreadsheet form will also provide greater flexibility to perform any analysis that a store manager might request of a salesperson.

Assignment

1. Based on the description above and the database file provided, generate an appropriate set of analysis and design aids for this application. Using these aids, develop a database application meeting all the requirements of this case. Test your application for accuracy and completeness.

2. Write an appropriate set of documentation to accompany your application. Be sure that your documentation fully describes all of the procedures needed to operate this application including appropriate control and back-up procedures.

3. Based on the sample data, can you see stockage adjustments that need to be made? Write a brief report summarizing adjustments to stockage levels that you would propose based upon the sample data. Attach copies of the reports you generated and use them to justify your proposed stockage adjustments.

Database Cases
151

CASE 10: Pace Picnic Products

Pace Picnic Products is a small scale manufacturer of plastic products. Pace produces plastic picnic supplies including plates, cups, tablecloths, and knives, forks, and spoons. The majority of Pace's sales are of disposable supplies. However, Pace also produces a line of heavy duty plastic picnic supplies designed for repeated use and this has been Pace's fastest growing product line in recent years.

Pace's products are all produced at a single factory in the midwest. At this factory there are a number of production lines. Distinct and different production lines are used for the manufacture of tablecloths, plates, cups, and utensils. The utensil production lines can produce any type of utensil: knife, fork, or spoon. Also, any of the production lines can be shifted from producing the lighter, disposable line, to producing the heavy duty, reusable, line of products. The production lines at Pace Picnic Products normally run 24 hours a day 5 days a week. Changes to machinery required to switch production from one type of utensil to another, or from light duty to heavy duty products, are time consuming. For that reason, production runs are planned so that each line produces a particular product through an entire work week. Changes required to produce a different utensil or weight of product are made while the plant is shut down over the weekend.

Mel Wells is the Director of Product Testing at Pace Plastic Products. His staff gathers samples of the output of each production line several times during each shift and tests the samples for quality and strength. At the end of each shift the number of units tested and the number of defective units found on each line are recorded. Mel's staff also records the total output of each production line for each shift. This information is kept in manual form until the end of the week. At the completion of each week, the production and inspection information for each shift on each production line is summed across the days of the week to produce a weekly Production and Quality Report which is transmitted to the IS Department and recorded in computerized form. An example of this form is shown below.

```
         PRODUCTION AND QUALITY REPORT
       Production Week: 23

                                       Units     Defective
  Line   Product   Shift   Output     Tested       Units

   A1   Forks-L    Day    187,360     1470          36
   A1   Forks-L    Eve.   193,284     1502          48
   A1   Forks-L    Ngt.   179,347     1398          29
   B2   Plates-H   Day     92,307     1106          26
    .      .         .        .          .            .
```

Data are recorded in the organizational database only on a weekly basis because, until recently, the inspections were performed much less frequently and product pulled from several days of production on a line was often pooled into a single inspection group. Thus, it was impossible to produce meaningful daily inspection data for each shift and line. Since the inspection data can now be meaningfully recorded on a daily basis, Mel Wells and the shift foremen would like to have daily shift performance information available in computerized form.

Mel submitted a proposal to Pace's IS Steering Committee for the conversion of this system to a daily recording and reporting basis. Because of a substantial applications backlog, the IS Steering Committee has adopted a policy of encouraging end user development of applications. When they reviewed Mel's proposal they indicated that the IS Department would not be able to perform this conversion for at least 18 months. However, they suggested that Mel consider end user development of his application.

Mel Wells has asked you to develop a prototype of this application for him. He indicates that the application should record production level and inspection results for each line in computerized form immediately at the end of each shift. The application should generate the Weekly Production and Quality Report that is submitted to the IS Department. This will cut down on employee time spent computing weekly totals and eliminate manual computation errors.

Beyond this routine output, Mel would like your application to be able to

Database Cases 153

produce a report at the end of each week which would compare production on a given production line across shifts and days of the week. Because different lines produce products with different expected levels of output and defect rates, one weekly report of this type would be produced for each line and no comparisons across lines would be used. Mel would like this report to include a calculation of the average output and average defect rate across the entire production week, where the defect rate for a given shift-day is simply the percentage of tested units that are defective. Mel also wants the report to include comparisons of each shift-day's performance to those averages. In other words, this report should compute the average of output and the defect rate across all shifts and days of the week and add a column comparing the levels for each particular shift-day to those averages. The comparisons to average would then be expressed in percentage terms. Thus, if average output per shift-day is 12,000 units and the output for the evening shift on Tuesday is 12,600, then production for the Tuesday evening shift is 105% of average.

Mel provides you with the set of sample data shown below for your use in developing a prototype of this application. He indicates that when the application becomes operational the inspectors on each shift will enter their shifts data each day, but that he will personally operate the application to produce the outputs he has described. Mel Wells is an experienced user of PC spreadsheets and database software, but many of his inspectors have no prior computing experience.

Sample Production and Inspection Data

Line	Product	Prod. Week	Day	Shift	Output	Units Tested	Defective Units
B2	Plates-H	23	Mon	Ngt.	90,640	1,076	33
B2	Plates-H	23	Mon	Day	92,347	1,102	29
B2	Plates-H	23	Mon	Eve.	91,823	1,053	33
B2	Plates-H	23	Tue	Ngt.	92,346	1,023	23
B2	Plates-H	23	Tue	Day	93,108	1,117	21
B2	Plates-H	23	Tue	Eve.	92,573	1,094	28
B2	Plates-H	23	Wed	Ngt.	88,643	1,023	33
B2	Plates-H	23	Wed	Day	93,807	1,005	24
B2	Plates-H	23	Wed	Eve.	91,654	1,106	29
B2	Plates-H	23	Thu	Ngt.	94,214	1,032	32
B2	Plates-H	23	Thu	Day	91,707	1,017	24
B2	Plates-H	23	Thu	Eve.	92,084	1,059	29
B2	Plates-H	23	Fri	Ngt.	93,107	1,034	35
B2	Plates-H	23	Fri	Day	90,008	1,008	31
B2	Plates-H	23	Fri	Eve.	88,730	1,117	39

Application Development Notes

Your first step in developing the application for this case should be to perform analysis and design activities and generate an appropriate set of analysis and design aids for use in implementing your application. The design and creation of a database table structure is an important part of this case. Based upon the description above and the sample data shown, you should develop a data dictionary form for these data and use its specification in creating your database table. Once your table structure has been created, you will need to enter the sample data shown above. An appropriate index should be created and maintained to sort the data by shift. Data will need to be sorted by shift for each of the reports in this application. The Weekly Production and Quality Report can be generated as a summary database report. However, data for each production line across all shifts and days of the week should be linked into a spreadsheet file for production of the report comparing each shift and day to average production levels and defect rates, since comparisons to average are not directly supported by most PC database packages.

Assignment

1. Based on the description above and the database file provided, generate an appropriate set of analysis and design aids for this application. Using these aids, develop a database application meeting all the requirements of this case. Test your application for accuracy and completeness.

2. Write an appropriate set of documentation to accompany your application. Be sure that your documentation fully describes all of the procedures needed to operate this application including appropriate control and back-up procedures.

3. Do you think that this is an appropriate application for end user development? Does this application create important organizational data that could be useful to a variety of individuals within the organization? Could this application be extended and eventually be incorporated into an organizational database? Write a brief discussion paper assessing these issues.

Data Dictionary

Table Name: PACE